your
leisure

EXPRESS NEWSPAPERS

non-retirement guides

your
leisure

Inspirational ideas for occupying your time

Edited by Frances Kay

**KOGAN
PAGE**

Publisher's note

Every possible effort has been made to ensure that the information contained in this book is accurate at the time of going to press, and the publishers and the author cannot accept responsibility for any errors or omissions, however caused. No responsibility for loss or damage occasioned to any person acting, or refraining from action, as a result of the material in this publication can be accepted by the editor, the publisher or the author.

First published in Great Britain in 2009 by Kogan Page Limited

Kogan Page Limited
120 Pentonville Road
London N1 9JN
United Kingdom
www.koganpage.com

© Kogan Page, 2009

British Library Cataloguing in Publication Data

A CIP record for this book is available from the British Library.

ISBN 978 0 7494 5587 3

Typeset by Jean Cussons Typesetting, Diss, Norfolk
Printed and bound in Great Britain by MPG Books Ltd, Bodmin, Cornwall

Contents

Introduction

Now that retirement is approaching, or has already arrived, are you looking forward to all that free time you will have? Some people (who take their retirement seriously) have made lists of all the things they are going to do, once the daily commute or work routine has ceased. Depending on your sphere of interest, there are more opportunities than time available to pursue hobbies, travel to new places, take up sport activities or volunteering. Most people over 60 wonder how they ever found time to go to work. The over-55s are a growth industry; current statistics show that there are far fewer under-16-year-olds in comparison. As a result, the choice of leisure pursuits is enormous. No wonder that there are endless opportunities for almost every kind of leisure activity. The only problem is likely to be fitting everything in.

The first section deals with spare-time activities, the second with sport and the third section relates to holidays. But all are inter-related. Many holidays involve special interest groups and tours, while other hobbies and pastimes involve short courses or visits to places of interest. Additionally, there are volunteering opportunities for retired people who wish to make a valuable contribution within their own community or beyond. You might consider visiting the elderly in their own homes, drive patients to hospital, run a holiday play scheme, help out at your local Citizens Advice Bureau or become a Samaritan. Other ideas that might appeal are conservation work or playing a more active role in politics by joining your local party association. Whether you can spare only the occasional day or can help on a regular basis, there are many suggestions you might like to consider.

Most organisations offer special concessionary rates to people of retirement age, as do a number of theatres and other places of entertainment. Given the immense variety of tantalising options on offer, it is perhaps no wonder that many retired people find that they have never been as busy in their lives.

1

Adult education and creative pursuits

Have you ever longed to take a degree, learn about computing, study philosophy or do a course in archaeology? Opportunities for education abound with these and there are scores of other subjects easily available to everyone, regardless of age or previous qualifications.

Adult education institutes

There is an adult education institute (AEI) in most areas of the country. Classes normally start in September and run through the academic year. Many AEIs allow concessionary fees for students over 60. Despite some recent cutbacks, the choice of subjects is still enormous; at one institute alone there were over 50 options, ranging from Indian history, video production and creative writing to self-defence, calligraphy, dressmaking and drama. Ask at your local library for details. For courses in London, consult Floodlight: website www.floodlight.co.uk. The following websites give further information: www.learndirect-advice.co.uk or www.direct.gov.uk.

National Adult School Organisation (NASO) promotes 'Conversation with a Purpose' through friendly discussion groups, meeting at places and times to suit their members. They follow either the NASO Handbook programme, topics of their own choice or a mixture of the two. Social activities and weekend conferences are organised regionally. For information about your nearest group contact NASO's General Secretary: Tel: 0116 253 8333; e-mail: GenSec@ naso.org.uk; website: www.naso.org.uk.

National Extension College (NEC) was set up over 40 years ago as a not-for-profit organisation to help people of all ages fit learning into their lives. Many of NEC's most able students are retired and are returning to study after many years. There is a choice of over 100 courses including GCSE and A level studies, personal development, childcare, bookkeeping, creative writing, arts, modern languages, counselling and many others. A student adviser can offer guidance on any aspect of your study plans and help you make an appropriate choice. Cost (2008/09) is upwards of £130 depending on which course you select. Contact: Tel: 0800 389 2839; e-mail: info@nec.ac.uk; website: www.nec. ac.uk.

Open and Distance Learning Quality Council (ODLQC) provide home study, distance learning, online or e-learning and other open learning or flexible learning courses. Their list includes colleges that teach your chosen subject, plus general advice on open and distance learning courses. The choice of subjects is enormous and, as well as academic and business subjects, includes such options as art, creative writing, graphology, needlework and sailing. Contact ODLQC on Tel: 020 7612 7090; e-mail: info@odlqc.org.uk; website: www.odlqc.org.uk.

Open University (OU). Why not take a degree or other qualification through The Open University? Students are all ages – the oldest OU graduate was 92 – most courses require no academic qualifications and there is a wide range of subjects from which to choose. Courses normally involve a mix of correspondence work, online learning, CDs and DVDs, and contact with local tutors. Some courses have a residential school. You can study at your own speed: on average people take up to six or eight years to get a degree. However, there is no long-term commitment and, if you wish, you can just sign on for one course.

The Open University also offers a range of short courses that are designed to give you a flavour of OU study if you want to try out a subject before committing yourself to a longer course. As well as being interesting in their own right, they can count towards an Open University degree, if you wish to continue. Fees range from around £125 for a short course to in excess of £500 for a standard nine-month course. Individuals who would have difficulty in paying may be eligible for financial support. There are also special allowances (DSAs) available to students who might be prevented from studying because of a disability, to help with the extra costs of services and facilities. Contact the OU on Tel: 0845 300 60 90; website: www.open.ac.uk.

Television and radio

The BBC is very involved on the learning front. **BBC Active** has a huge catalogue of educational programmes that are available for institutional use, or for students and those doing personal research. Many programmes have accompanying books as well as CDs and DVDs. Contact BBC Active by e-mail: bbcactive.bbcstudies@pearson.com; website: www.bbcactive.com.

University extra-mural departments – non-degree and short courses

Many universities have a Department of Extra-Mural Studies that arranges courses for adults, sometimes in the evening or during vacation periods. For example, the Faculty of Lifelong Learning, **Birkbeck, University of London,** offers over 1,000 part-time courses in a range of subjects, including literature and drama, music, philosophy, history, sociology and psychology. Classes normally meet once a week and students are required to do reading and written work. Fees vary according to the length of the course and many offer concessions to those whose main source of income is a State pension or government benefit. For further information Tel: 0845 601 0174; e-mail: info@bbk.ac.uk; website: www.bbk.ac.uk. For other universities, enquire locally.

The Third Age Trust, U3A (The University of The Third Age) is a self-help movement for people no longer in full-time employment, offering a wide range of educational, creative and leisure activities. It operates through a national network of local U3As, each of which determines its own courses and social programmes according to the interests of its members. There is also a national magazine *U3A News*, which is published four times a year. For a brochure, together with a list of names and addresses of all local U3As contact: Tel: 020 8466 6139; e-mail: national.office@ u3a.org.uk; website: www.u3a.org.uk.

Workers' Educational Association (WEA) is the United Kingdom's largest voluntary sector provider of adult learning. Founded over 100 years ago, its members come from all walks of life, and share a belief in the value of education and lifelong learning for all adults regardless of circumstance. It offers a wide range of courses including education for retirement. Currently there are over 19,000 members. Membership is free in England, in Scotland it is £3.00 annually. For further information contact the National Membership Department, WEA: Tel: 020 7426 3450; e-mail: membership@wea.org.uk; website: www.wea. org.uk.

Animals

If you are an animal lover, you will already know about such events as sheepdog trials and gymkhanas, and the many wildlife sanctuaries around the country. Our list is effectively limited to 'the birds and the bees' with just a couple of extra suggestions for fun.

British Beekeepers' Association runs correspondence courses and practical demonstrations and will be glad to put you in touch with one of the 60 local organisations. Tel: 0247 669 6679; website: www.britishbee.org.uk.

Our Dogs Publishing has information if you would enjoy showing a dog. The weekly newspaper *Our Dogs* gives details of local shows, rule and registration changes and also news and addresses of canine and breed societies all over the country. There is an Our Dogs diary, which contains feeding and other hints, advice about the Kennel Club and much other useful information. Contact Our Dogs on Tel: 0870 731 6503; email: subs@ourdogs.co.uk; website: www.ourdogs.co.uk.

Wildfowl & Wetlands Trust (WWT) works to conserve threatened wetland birds and their habitats. In addition to Slimbridge, there are visitor centres in Lancashire, Sussex, Tyne & Wear, the Cambridgeshire/Norfolk Border, London, Dumfriesshire, South Wales and Northern Ireland. Membership (2008–09) costs £33.00 for a single adult, £24 for a single concession, and gives you free entry to all WWT centres plus receipt of the quarterly magazine. There is wheelchair access to all centres, grounds and many hides. For further information contact WWT at Tel: 01453

891900; e-mail: enquiries@wwt.org.uk; website: www.wwt. org.uk.

Arts

Enjoyment of the arts is certainly no longer confined to London. Whether you are interested in active participation or just appreciating the performance of others, there is an exhilarating choice of events, including theatre, music, exhibitions, film-making and so on. Many entertainments offer concessionary prices to retired people.

Regional arts council offices

For first-hand information about what is going on in your area, contact your regional arts council office (see national website); or in the case of those living in Scotland, Wales and Northern Ireland, the national arts council. Most areas arrange an immensely varied programme with musical events, drama, arts and craft exhibitions and sometimes more unusual functions, offering something of interest to just about everyone. Many regional arts councils produce regular newsletters with information for their area.

Arts Council England, East. Area covered: Bedfordshire, Cambridgeshire, Essex, Hertfordshire, Norfolk, Suffolk; and unitary authorities of Luton, Peterborough, Southend-on-Sea, and Thurrock.

Arts Council England, East Midlands. Area covered: Derbyshire, Leicestershire, Lincolnshire (excluding North and North East Lincolnshire), Northamptonshire, Nottinghamshire; and unitary authorities of Derby, Leicester, Nottingham, and Rutland.

Arts Council England, London. Area covered: Greater London.

Arts Council England, North East. Area covered: Durham, Northumberland; metropolitan authorities of Gateshead, Newcastle-upon-Tyne, North Tyneside, South Tyneside, Sunderland; and unitary authorities of Darlington, Hartlepool, Middlesbrough, Redcar and Cleveland, and Stockton-on-Tees.

Arts Council England, North West. Area covered: Cheshire, Cumbria, Lancashire; metropolitan authorities of Bolton, Bury, Knowsley, Liverpool, Manchester, Oldham, Rochdale, St Helens, Salford, Sefton, Stockport, Tameside, Trafford, Wigan, Wirral; and unitary authorities of Blackburn with Darwen, Blackpool, Halton, and Warrington.

Arts Council England, South East. Area covered: Buckinghamshire, East Sussex, Hampshire, Isle of Wight, Kent, Oxfordshire, Surrey, West Sussex; and unitary authorities of Bracknell Forest, Brighton and Hove, Medway Towns, Milton Keynes, Portsmouth, Reading, Slough, Southampton, West Berkshire, Windsor and Maidenhead, and Wokingham.

Arts Council England, South West. Area covered: Cornwall, Devon, Dorset, Gloucestershire, Somerset, Wiltshire; unitary authorities of Bath and North East Somerset, Bournemouth, Bristol, North Somerset, Plymouth, Poole, South Gloucestershire, Swindon, and Torbay.

Arts Council England, West Midlands. Area covered: Shropshire, Staffordshire, Warwickshire, Worcestershire; metropolitan authorities of Birmingham, Coventry, Dudley, Sandwell, Solihull, Walsall, Wolverhampton; and unitary authorities of Herefordshire, Stoke-on-Trent, Telford and Wrekin.

Arts Council England, Yorkshire. Area covered: North Yorkshire; metropolitan authorities of Barnsley, Bradford, Calderdale, Doncaster, Kirklees, Leeds, Rotherham, Sheffield, Wakefield; and unitary authorities of East Riding of Yorkshire, Kingston upon Hull, North Lincolnshire, North East Lincolnshire, and York.

For all **Arts Council** offices, contact Tel: 0845 300 6200; e-mail: enquiries@artscouncil.org.uk; website: www.arts council.org.uk.

For those who wish to join in with amateur arts activities, public libraries keep lists of choirs, drama clubs, painting clubs and similar activities in their locality.

Films

The cinema is hugely popular as an art form. If the only films showing in your area are the latest releases, you might think of joining a film society or perhaps taking a trip to the National Film Theatre to view some of the great performances of the past or to see some of the excellent foreign films that are rarely shown out of London.

British Federation of Film Societies (BFFS) – Cinema for All. BFFS is the national organisation for the development, support and representation of film societies (of which there are over 300) throughout the United Kingdom. Most offer reduced rates for senior citizens. Contact details can be obtained from BFFS. If, as a growing number of people are, you are interested in forming a local film society with a group of friends and neighbours, contact the BFFS Central Office for information on equipment, money and how to get started. Tel: 0114 221 0314; e-mail: info@bffs.org.uk; website: www.bffs.org.uk.

BFI Southbank shows some 2,000 films a year at the BFI's three cinemas. Box Office booking line: Tel: 020 7928 3232. **British Film Institute** membership, from £20 annually, is available from the BFI. Contact: Tel: 020 7815 1374; website: www.bfi.org.uk.

Music and ballet

Scope ranges from becoming a Friend and supporting one of the famous 'Houses' such as Covent Garden to music-making in your own right. If you live close enough to take advantage of the 'perks', subscribing as a Friend allows you a number of very attractive advantages, including in all cases priority for bookings.

Friends of Covent Garden. Friends receive regular mailings of news and information, and free copies of the magazine

About the House, plus opportunities to attend talks, recitals, study days, master classes and some 'open' rehearsals of ballet and opera. Annual membership is £78. For further details: Tel: 020 7212 9268; e-mail: friends@roh.org.uk; website: www.royalopera.org.

Friends of English National Opera. As a Friend of ENO, you have the opportunity to apply for tickets for dress rehearsals and to gain an insight into the creation of opera through a variety of special lunchtime and evening events. You also receive advance programme information. Membership (2008) is £50 a year. For further information and full details contact: Tel: 0871 271 5577; e-mail: friends@eno.org; website: www.eno.org.

Friends of Sadler's Wells. Sadler's Wells has an ever-changing programme of ballet, opera and contemporary dance. Friends receive discounts and free ticket offers. Annual membership is £100. For further details: Tel: 020 7863 8134; e-mail: membership@sadlerswells.com; website: www.sadlerswells.com.

Music making

Just about every style of music is catered for, from bell-ringing to recorder playing. There is even an orchestra for retired people.

Handbell Ringers of Great Britain. The Society, which was formed in 1967, promotes the art of handbell tune ringing and supports handbell, handchime and belleplate players. Concerts, rallies, seminars and workshops are organised.

General enquiries should be made through the National Secretary: e-mail: sandra@hrgb.org.uk; website: www.hrgb. org.uk.

Making Music, The National Federation of Music Societies, can provide you with addresses of some 2,000 affiliated choral societies, orchestras and music societies throughout the country. Most charge a nominal membership fee and standards range from the semi-professional to the unashamedly amateur. For further details contact: Tel: 020 7422 8280; e-mail: info@makingmusic.org.uk; website: www.makingmusic.org.uk.

National Association of Choirs. The Association will put you in contact with an amateur choir in your area. Contact: Tel: 0870 760 7356; e-mail: rhodeswf@ntlworld.com; website: www.ukchoirsassoc.co.uk.

Society of Recorder Players. The Society has groups in many areas, where members play together regularly. The branches welcome players of all standards and ages but do not provide tuition for beginners. There is an annual festival with massed playing, competitions and concerts. For details contact the Membership Secretary: Tel: 01706 853312; e-mail: memsec@srp.org.uk; website: www.srp.org.uk.

Poetry

Poetry used to be a minority interest. However, largely thanks to both the media and the Poetry Society, there has been an increase in enthusiasm about poetry and poetry readings in clubs, pubs and other places of entertainment.

Your library should be able to tell you about any special local events.

The Poetry Society. Membership of the Society is open to anyone who enjoys reading, listening to or writing poetry. The Society runs a poetry criticism service where, for an agreed fee, you can have your work assessed. Each year the Society organises a National Poetry Competition with a first prize of £5,000. Additionally, members receive the Society's quarterly magazines *Poetry Review and Poetry News*. Annual subscription (2008) is £30 concession. For further details, contact: Tel: 020 7420 9880; e-mail: info@poetry society.org.uk; website: www.poetrysociety.org.uk.

Television and radio audiences

If you would like to be part of the invited studio audience for a BBC radio or television programme you can apply to: **BBC Radio and Television Studio Audiences,** contact: Tel: 0870 901 1227; website: www.bbc.co.uk/tickets.

Ticket information for outside London programmes should normally be obtainable from the programme direct or via the local BBC studio/office.

For independent television channels, information can be obtained by contacting:

ITV Viewer Enquiries. Contact: Tel: 0844 881 4150; email: bookings@lostintv.com; websites: www.itv.com; www.itv local.com.

Channel 4 Viewers Enquiries. Contact: Tel: 0845 076 0191; website: www.channel4.com.

Ulster TV. Contact: Tel: 028 9032 8122; website: www. ulstertv.com.

Theatre

Details of current and forthcoming productions, as well as theatre reviews, are contained in the newspapers. Preview performances are usually cheaper and there are often concessionary tickets for matinees. Listed here are some theatres and organisations that offer special facilities of interest, including priority booking and reduced price tickets. Also included is an association for enthusiasts of amateur dramatics.

Barbican Centre. The Barbican Centre combines two theatres, a concert hall, two art galleries, three cinemas and a library. There are frequent free live musical events in the foyers, free exhibitions and restaurant facilities. Reduced tickets for senior citizens are available for many concerts and theatre performances and are also given for the art gallery and cinema. For £20 a year, members receive a monthly guide and enjoy advance information and special offers for theatre, music and other events. Contact: Tel: 0845 121 6823; e-mail: tickets@barbican.org.uk; website: www.barbican.org.uk.

National Theatre. The National Theatre offers backstage tours, talks by theatre professionals, live foyer music before performances, free exhibitions, and restaurant facilities as well as its three theatres. There are group price reductions and pensioners can also buy midweek matinee tickets at concessionary prices. The National Theatre has a Mailing List Membership (£10 a year for senior citizens) that provides advance information, priority booking and exclusive special offers. For details, contact: Tel: 020 7452 3500 (10 am to 6 pm, Monday to Friday); e-mail: advance@ nationaltheatre.org.uk; website: www.nationaltheatre.org. uk.

Society of London Theatre (SOLT). Senior citizens can get substantial reductions for midweek matinee performances at many West End theatres. They can also receive concessionary prices for evening performances or weekend mat inees on a standby basis with all listings showing the symbol 'S' in the *London Theatre Guide*. Standby tickets are available approximately an hour before the performance begins. Concessions are subject to availability and it is always wise to check with the box office to make sure there are tickets before setting off for a performance. When buying tickets on a concessionary basis, you will need to present proof of your senior citizen status at the box office; for example, using a travel pass or pension book.

Theatre Tokens, which are welcome at over 235 theatres nationwide including all London West End theatres, are available by calling **Tokenline**: Tel: 0870 164 8800; or via the website: www.theatretokens.com.

Also extremely useful is the Society's *Disabled Access Guide to London West End Theatres*, which provides information about special facilities, access for wheelchairs, transport advice and price concessions for disabled theatergoers, and is available free from SOLT. Contact details: Tel: 020 7557 6700; e-mail: enquiries@solttma.co.uk; website: www. officiallondontheatre.co.uk.

Scottish Community Drama Association aims to develop amateur drama in the community by offering clubs and societies advice, encouragement and practical help. Individual membership (£23 adult, £18 concession) gives access to the Association's libraries, training courses and script discounts. The Association also runs playwriting competitions and can put you in touch with local dramatic societies. Members receive regular copies of the house magazine. Contact: Tel: 0131 557 5552; e-mail: headquarters@scda.org.uk; website: www.scda.org.uk.

TKTS, run by the Society of London Theatres, is a booth, located in Leicester Square, selling tickets to many West End theatres at half price on the day of the performance. It is open to personal callers only, Monday to Saturday, from 10 am to 7 pm, and on Sundays from 12 noon to 3 pm. In the case of matinees, it is open for ticket sales until half an hour before starting time. There is a service charge of £2.50 per ticket. Website: www.officiallondontheatre.co.uk.

Visual arts

If you enjoy attending exhibitions and lectures, membership of some of the arts societies offers you a number of delightful privileges.

The Art Fund raises money to help museums, galleries and historic houses buy works of art to enrich their collections.

The benefits of membership include: free entrance to over 200 museums and galleries; half-price admission to major exhibitions; a countrywide programme of lectures, concerts, private views and other special events, including visits to houses not normally open to the public; *Art Quarterly* magazine; plus an illustrated review of the year's acquisitions. There are also art tours at home and abroad led by experts. Subscription is from £30 per year single and from £37.50 per couple. For further information, contact: Tel: 0870 848 2003; e-mail: members@artfund.org; website: www.artfund.org.

Contemporary Art Society. The aim of the Society is to promote the collecting of contemporary art and to acquire works by living artists for gift to public galleries. Members can take part in an extensive programme of events including visits to artists' studios and private collections, previews and parties at special exhibitions, and trips outside London and overseas. All events are free. The subscription (2008) for normal membership plus one guest is £275; distance membership plus one guest is £225. Contact: Tel: 020 7831 1243; e-mail: cas@contempart.org.uk; website: www. con tempart.org.uk.

National Association of Decorative & Fine Arts Societies. Member societies of NADFAS have programmes of monthly lectures, museum and gallery visits, as well as guided tours of historic houses. Many societies have volunteer groups working in museums, libraries and historic houses and there are also church-recording groups that make detailed records of the interiors of churches. Details of your local society are available from NADFAS (see website). Membership of a local society is about £30–50 a year. It gives access to nationally run study courses, a quarterly magazine and reduced entry to some galleries, plus the opportunity to join day events and tours organised both in the United Kingdom and abroad. Contact NADFAS at Tel: 020 7430 0730; e-mail: enquiries@nadfas.org.uk; website: www.nadfas.org.uk.

Royal Academy of Arts. Senior citizens enjoy reduced entrance charges to all exhibitions, including the big annual Summer Exhibition. You can become a Friend of the Royal Academy, which gives you free admission to all exhibitions with an adult guest and up to four family children under 16. Friends may also use the Friends' Rooms to meet for coffee and attend exhibition previews. Subscription (2008) is £76 a year single membership (or if paying by direct debit or major credit card £66), and £110 joint membership (or £100 if paying by direct debit or credit card). For further information: Tel: 020 7300 5664; e-mail: friend.enquiries@royal academy.org.uk; website: www.royalacademy.org.uk.

Tate Britain and Tate Modern. London now boasts two magnificent Tate galleries: Tate Britain at Millbank, which houses the most important collection of British art from 1500 to the present day; and Tate Modern, on the site of the Bankside Power Station at Southwark, which contains international 20th- and 21st-century art, including works by Giacometti, Picasso and Warhol. There are free weekly lectures and guided tours every day, except Sunday; also special tours for disabled people by prior arrangement. Tate members enjoy free admission to all exhibitions, receipt of *Tate Magazine* and access to the Members' Room, including those at Tate Liverpool and Tate St Ives. For further information, contact: Tel: 020 7887 8888; e-mail: members@ tate.org.uk; website: www.tate.org.uk.

Painting as a hobby

If you are interested in improving your own painting technique, rather than simply viewing the works of great masters, art courses are available at your local adult education institute. See 'Adult education institutes' at the beginning of this chapter. Your library may have details of painting groups and societies in your area.

Crafts

Crafts Council runs an information centre and reference library that can give advice on almost everything you could possibly want to know: different craft courses throughout the country, addresses of craft guilds and societies, fact-sheets on business practice for craftspeople as well as details of craft fairs and markets, galleries, shops and other outlets for work. Additionally, the Crafts Council has a slide, video and DVD library, publishes a bimonthly magazine, *Crafts*, and maintains an index of craftspeople and the national register of makers. For further information contact: Tel: 020 7806 2500; website: www.crafts council.org.uk.

Open College of the Arts (OCA), which is affiliated to the Open University, offers home study courses for those wishing to acquire or improve their skills or gain a Higher Education qualification. Courses offered include creative digital arts, sculpture, textiles, art and design, creative writing and photography. Course books are supplied and students have professional tutorial support from artists, writers and designers. Courses cost from around £450. For further information and a free *Guide to Courses*, contact: Tel: 0800 731 2116; e-mail: enquiries@oca-uk.com; website: www.oca-uk.com.

Dance/keep fit

Clubs, classes and groups exist in all parts of the country, variously offering ballroom, Old Tyme, Scottish, folk, ballet, disco dancing and others. Additionally, there are music and relaxation classes, aerobics and more gentle keep-fit sessions. Many of the relaxation and keep-fit classes in particular cater for all standards. Some are specially designed for older people to tone up muscles and improve their circulation, while making friends in an agreeable atmosphere. Best advice is to contact your adult education or sports centre. Alternatively, the library may help you to find out what is available in your area. Listed here are some of the national organisations that can advise you and put you in touch with local groups.

British Dance Council. The Council, which is the governing body of ballroom dancing in Great Britain, can put you in touch with recognised dance schools in your area. Contact the Secretary: Tel: 020 8545 0085; e-mail: secretary@british-dance-council.org; website: www.british-dance-council.org.

The CCPR One Voice for Sport and Recreation. The CCPR represents over 270 governing and representative bodies in the sport and recreation sectors. For more information contact the CCPR: Tel: 020 7976 3900; e-mail: info@ccpr.org.uk; website: www.ccpr.org.uk.

English Folk Dance and Song Society. There are some 590 clubs around the country that organise both regular and special events. In addition to ordinary folk dancing, programmes may include country dancing, morris dancing, 'knees-up', clog workshops, musician band sessions, sea shanties, lectures and concerts. Membership (2008), which includes journals and use of the library, costs £36 single, £55 joint; concessions £22 single, £36 joint. Contact the Society for details of your nearest group: Tel: 020 7485 2206; e-mail: info@efdss.org; website: www.efdss.org.

Imperial Society of Teachers of Dancing. Throughout the United Kingdom there are some 7,000 teachers offering instruction in virtually all forms of dancing; many organise classes and events, particularly for older people. The Society has lists of teachers in each geographic area. There is no standard charge but dance classes and social dancing tend to be inexpensive activities. For further details contact: Tel: 020 7377 1577; e-mail: membership@istd.org; website: www. istd.org.

Keep Fit Association (KFA). The Keep Fit Association offers 'Fitness through Movement, Exercise and Dance' classes, suitable for all ages and abilities. KFA teachers have special training in working with older people. Almost all adult education centres run classes in the daytime; many have special classes for keeping fit in retirement. For more information: Tel: 01403 266000; e-mail: kfa@keepfit.org.uk; website: www.keepfit.org.uk.

Royal Scottish Country Dance Society has members from 16 to 80-plus in its many branches and groups all over the world. It publishes books, CDs and DVDs, and holds an annual summer school at St Andrew's University. The branches offer instruction at all levels and members join in dance events. Information about your local branch/group can be obtained by contacting: Tel: 0131 225 3854; e-mail: info@rscds.org; website: www.rscds.org.

Games

Many local areas have their own bridge, chess, whist, dominoes, Scrabble and other groups who meet together regularly, in either a club, hall, pub or other social venue to enjoy friendly games. Competitions are organised and, certainly in the case of bridge and chess, district and county teams are usually taken very seriously. Your library should know about any clubs or regular group meetings. Alternatively, you can contact the national organisations listed below.

English Bridge Union has details of over 1,000 affiliated bridge clubs nationwide. Members receive a wide range of services including a free diary, discounts on cards and other bridge items and six magazines a year, which among other features of interest contain details of tournaments and bridge holidays at home and abroad. For further information contact: Tel: 01296 317200; e-mail: postmaster@ebu.co.uk; website: www.ebu.co.uk.

English Chess Federation can provide information about chess clubs and tournaments throughout the country. Contact: Tel: 01424 775222; e-mail: office@englishchess.org.uk; website: www.englishchess.org.uk.

Scrabble Clubs UK. There are over 300 Scrabble clubs up and down the country. Some have their own premises and are highly competitive. Others meet in halls or members' houses for a friendly game. Many of them are involved in charitable work, such as raising money for people with disabilities or visiting the housebound. Many competitions are held, including a National Scrabble Championship and a big tournament for clubs. For details of your nearest Scrabble club, contact the Secretary: email: anne.ramsay@ blueyonder.co.uk; website: www.absp.org.uk.

Gardens and gardening

Courses, gardens to visit, special help for people with disabilities, how to run a gardening association; these and other interests are all catered for by the organisations listed.

The English Gardening School teaches all aspects of gardening. Courses ranging in length from a day to an academic year are held in the lecture room of the historic Chelsea Physic Garden, a centre for the study of horticulture for over 300 years. Topics include: Garden design, container gardening, pruning roses, the mixed border and botanical illustration. Cost (2008) is from £125 for a day course, including lunch. For further information contact: Tel: 020 7352 4337; e-mail: info@egs.dircon.co.uk; website: www. englishgardeningschool.co.uk.

Gardening for Disabled Trust & Garden Club provides practical and financial help to disabled people who want to garden actively. Its Garden Club publishes a quarterly newsletter, gives answers to horticultural questions and encourages gardeners with disabilities to meet. The annual subscription (2008) is £5. Contact the Secretary: www. gardeningfordisabledtrust.org.uk.

Garden Organic is Europe's largest organic gardening organisation. It encourages environmentally friendly gardening and its centre is open to visitors throughout the year. One of the major attractions is the vegetable kingdom, which is a fully interactive visitor centre. Individuals can help by experimenting in their own gardens and joining a network of countrywide local groups. Members receive a quarterly magazine, a sales catalogue with discounts and gardening advice. Subscription (2008) at the concessionary rate is £20 single, £22 for a couple. For further information contact: Tel: 024 7630 3517; e-mail: enquiry@garden organic.org.uk; website: www.gardenorganic.org.uk.

National Gardens Scheme covers some 3,500 gardens, mostly privately owned, that open to the public a few days a year to raise money for a variety of nursing, caring and gardening charities including: Macmillan Cancer Relief, Marie Curie Cancer Care and the Queen's Nursing Institute. Tea is often available, as are plants for sale. For further information please contact: Tel: 01483 211535; e-mail: ngs@ngs.org.uk; website: www.ngs.org.uk.

National Society of Allotment and Leisure Gardeners Ltd. The Society encourages all forms of horticultural education and the forming of local allotment and gardening associations. It also acts as a national voice for allotment and leisure gardeners. Annual membership costs £15; society membership is £1.75 per member. This gives you access to free help and advice, and the right to attend the annual meeting, plus receipt of the Society's bulletin. There is also a Seeds Scheme, offering special prices. Leaflets are available on growing vegetables, how to form a gardening association and the running of flower shows. For further information contact: Tel: 01536 266576; e-mail: natsoc@nsalg.org.uk; website: www.nsalg.org.uk.

Royal Horticultural Society members enjoy free entry to over 130 gardens across Britain and privileged entry and reduced-rate tickets to RHS flower shows, including both Chelsea and Hampton Court Palace. They also receive a monthly copy of *The Garden* magazine and can use a free gardening advice service. Membership (2008) starts at £46. For further information contact: Tel: 0845 062 1111; e-mail: membership@rhs.org.uk; website: www.rhs.org.uk.

Scotland's Gardens Scheme supports retired Queen's Nurses, the Gardens Fund of the National Trust for Scotland and other charities through 360 gardens that are open to the public either on one day only or on a regular basis. The booklet giving opening times is available from all main retail outlets or by contacting Tel: 0131 226 3714; e-mail: info@sgsgardens.co.uk; website: www.gardensof scotland.org.

Thrive is a small national charity that uses gardening to change lives. It champions the benefits of gardening, carries out research and offers training and practical solutions so that anyone with a disability can take part in, benefit from and enjoy gardening. It will give advice about special tools and where these can be obtained. Thrive also runs garden projects based in Battersea Park, London SW11, and Beech

Hill, near Reading, Berkshire. Contact: Tel: 0118 988 5688; website: www.thrive.org.uk.

Useful reading

Getting on with Gardening, Volumes 1 and 2, £7.50 each in clear print version or cassette version. An A4 ring binder with inserts is included in the price. Available from RNIB Customer Services: Tel: 0845 702 3153; e-mail: CServices@ rnib.org.uk.

History

People with an interest in the past have a truly glorious choice of activities to sample. You can visit historic monuments, including ancient castles and stately homes, in all parts of the country; explore the City of London; study genealogy; research the history of your local area; attend lectures and receptions.

Age Exchange Reminiscence Centre features exhibitions recording the lifestyles of the 1920s and 1930s. There are also publications depicting the period, plus a year-round programme of activities for visitors to enjoy, including reminiscence through the arts, music and drama. The Centre is open Monday to Friday from 10 am to 5 pm, and on Saturday from 10 am to 4 pm. Admission is free. There is a small charge for group bookings. The Centre is fully equipped for disabled access and has a café serving light refreshments. Contact: Tel: 020 8318 9105; e-mail: adminis-

trator@age-exchange.org.uk; website: www.age-exchange.
org.uk.

Architectural Heritage Society of Scotland promotes the
protection of Scottish architecture and encourages the study
of Scottish buildings, their furniture and fittings, urban
design and designed landscapes. There are six regional
groups, covering all of Scotland, which arrange regular
events including talks, visits and study trips. Members can
also join case panels to assess Listed Building and
Conservation Area Consent applications and planning
applications. Annual membership (2008), including the
Society's publications, is £25; £35 for a family. Contact:
Tel: 0131 557 0019; e-mail: administrator@ahss.org.uk;
website: www.ahss.org.uk.

British Association for Local History exists to promote the
study of local history. It will give advice and invite you to
conferences and courses. Typical topics include introductory
days at the Public Record Office, computers in local history
and writing about your local area. Membership (2008),
which includes copies of both *The Local Historian and
Local History News*, is £25. Contact: Tel: 01283 585 947;
e-mail: mail@balh.co.uk; website: www.balh.co.uk.

City of London Information Centre acts as a tourist office
for the area, giving advice and guidance. Among the many
attractions, all of which are open to the public at varying
times, are: St Paul's Cathedral, the Guildhall (open most of
the year, Monday to Saturday, from 10 am to 4 pm, free), Dr
Johnson's House, the Monument, the Barbican, the Central
Criminal Court and several museums. Additionally, there
are interesting examples of London's architecture. Many of

the 43 churches give organ recitals and, in the summer, you can enjoy open-air concerts. The Centre offers lots of free leaflets, including the monthly events list. Contact: Tel: 020 7606 3030; e-mail: pro@cityoflondon.gov.uk; website: www.cityoflondon.gov.uk.

English Heritage manages over 400 historic attractions throughout England. Members receive a colour handbook with map (see below). They enjoy free admission to all English Heritage properties and are sent a quarterly magazine publicising events and developments of conservation interest. Annual subscription (2008) for a single adult is £42; for a single concession £30; couple concession is £60. These prices are valid to March 2009. *The English Heritage Visitors' Handbook* indicates which sites have access for wheelchairs. Contact: Tel: 0870 333 1182; e-mail: members@english-heritage.org.uk; website: www.english-heritage.org.uk.

Federation of Family History Societies is an umbrella organisation for more than 200 societies throughout the world (160 in the United Kingdom) that provide assistance if you are interested in tracing your ancestors. You can be put in touch with your local society, and obtain useful guidelines on how to get started. Contact: Tel: 01455 203 133; e-mail: info@ffhs.org.uk; website: www.ffhs.org.uk.

Friends of Historic Scotland. Membership gives you free access to 330 of Scotland's historic buildings and ancient monuments, a free directory of the sites and a quarterly magazine to keep you up to date with new activities. Membership (2008) costs £28 for senior citizens; £48 for retired couples. Contact: Tel: 0131 668 8999; website: www.stately-homes.com.

Garden History Society is concerned with the study, enjoyment and conservation of historic parks and gardens. It organises visits and lectures for members. An annual summer conference and foreign tours are also arranged. A journal, *Garden History*, is published twice a year and there are also regular newsletters. Subscriptions (2008) are £35 single; £43 joint. Contact: Tel: 020 7608 2409; e-mail: enquiries@gardenhistorysociety.org; website: www.gardenhistorysociety.org.

Georgian Group. The Group exists to preserve Georgian buildings and to stimulate public knowledge and appreciation of Georgian architecture and town planning. Activities include day visits and long weekends to buildings and gardens, private views of exhibitions and a programme of evening lectures in London. The Georgian Group also publishes advisory leaflets and holds study days on the history and conservation of Georgian buildings. Membership (2008) is £35 a year; £50 for couples. Contact: Tel: 0871 750 2936; e-mail: tina@georgiangroup.org.uk; website: www.georgiangroup.org.uk.

Historical Association. The Association brings together people of all ages and backgrounds who share an interest in and love for the past. Members receive *The Historian* (a fully illustrated quarterly magazine) and may join in a wide variety of activities such as lectures, outings, conferences and tours both at home and abroad conducted by expert lecturers. There are over 50 local branches nationwide offering a programme of social events and monthly talks by top historians. The Association also publishes a number of useful historical pamphlets. Membership (2008) costs £44.50 a year; £28 concession. Contact: T: 020 7735 3901; email: enquiry@history.org.uk; website: www.history.org.uk.

Historic Houses Association (HHA). Friends of the HHA enjoy access to nearly 300 HHA-member houses and gardens in England, Scotland and Wales and receive the quarterly magazine *Historic House* as well as invitations to lectures, concerts, receptions and other events. Subscription rates (2008) are individual £36, double £58. Contact: Tel: 01462 896 688; e-mail: hhafriends@hall-mccartney.co.uk; website: www.hha.org.uk.

Monumental Brass Society encourages the preservation and appreciation of monumental brasses. Members attend four meetings with lectures and discussions and receive three bulletins, the annual *Transactions*, and an invitation to the annual excursion/study day. Subscription is £25 a year. There are many brass-rubbing centres around the country where facilities are provided for the craft. Contact: Membership Secretary: e-mail: rmwillatts@tiscali.co.uk; website: www.mbs-brasses.co.uk.

National Trust. The National Trust exists to protect historic buildings and areas of great natural beauty in England, Wales and Northern Ireland. Membership gives you free entry to the Trust's many properties and to those of the National Trust for Scotland. You also receive three mailings with an annual handbook, magazines and details of activities in your own region. Thousands of special events are arranged each year, including guided house tours, pop and classical concerts, children's events and adult education activities. The Trust publishes a free annual booklet on facilities for visitors with disabilities; those requiring the help of a companion will be charged admission as normal but their companion will be admitted free of charge on request. The booklet is available from the membership department on receipt of a stamped addressed adhesive label (minimum postage). Membership rate for over-60s is £32 per year. Contact: Tel: 0844 800 1895; e-mail: enquiries@thenational trust.org.uk; website: www.nationaltrust.org.uk.

National Trust for Scotland. The National Trust for Scotland cares for over 100 properties and 183,000 acres of countryside. Members also enjoy free admission to any of the National Trust properties in England, Wales and Northern Ireland. Membership (2008) is £44 a year; senior citizens, £31; joint senior, £51. Contact: Tel: 0844 493 2100; email: information@nts.org.uk; website: www.nts. org.uk.

Northern Ireland Tourist Board. There is a free information bulletin, *Visitor Attractions*, listing historic sites and other places of interest. Many sites are free and others offer reduced rates for pensioners. An *Events* leaflet describes a selection of the most important, interesting or new events in Northern Ireland each year, such as music festivals, sporting occasions, agricultural shows and art exhibitions. Accommodation offers – including hotel breaks, self-catering holidays, guest houses and bed-and-breakfasts – are listed in the Short Breaks brochure, which offers year-round deals throughout Northern Ireland. Contact: Tel: 028 9023 1221; e-mail: info@nitb.com; website: www.discovernorthernireland.com.

Oral History Society. The Society offers support and advice to groups and individuals around the country who record the memories of older people for projects in community history, schools, reminiscence groups and historical research. It publishes twice-yearly journals and runs regular workshops and conferences. It welcomes the help of older people in all these activities. Individual membership is £20 a year. Contact the Membership Secretary: Tel: 020 7412 7405; e-mail: rob.perks@bl.uk; website: www.ohs.org.uk.

Society of Genealogists. The Society promotes the study of genealogy and heraldry. Lectures are arranged throughout the year and there are also a variety of courses, including day and weekend seminars. Members have access to the library and also receive a quarterly magazine. There is a joining fee of £10 and annual membership is £45. Non-members may use the library on payment of hourly, half-daily or daily fees. Contact: Tel: 020 7251 8799; e-mail: membership@sog.org.uk; website: www.sog.org.uk.

Victorian Society. The Victorian Society campaigns to preserve fine Victorian and Edwardian buildings. It organises walks, tours, lectures and conferences through its national office and eight regional groups. Membership (2008) is individual, £35; senior citizens, £25. Contact: Tel: 020 8994 1019; e-mail: admin@victoriansociety.org.uk; website: www.victorian-society.org.uk.

Special interests

Whether your special enthusiasm is stamp collecting or model flying, most of the following associations organise events, answer queries and can put you in contact with kindred spirits.

The British Association of Numismatic Societies (BANS) is an umbrella organisation that helps to coordinate the activities of some 50 local clubs for those interested in the study or collection of coins, medals or similar. It organises two conferences a year, maintains a slide library and will be able to put you in touch with your nearest group. Contact: Tel: 020 8523 6351; e-mail: phil_mernick@bushboakeallen. com; website: www.coinclubs.freeserve.co.uk.

British Jigsaw Puzzle Library. This is a lending library with puzzles usually exchanged by post. The puzzles are wooden and have no guide pictures. They vary in difficulty, style and size and the library tries to suit each member. Subscriptions range from £42 for three months to £105 for a year. Postal charges are extra. Contact: Tel: 01227 742222; e-mail: jigsawinfo@aol.com; website: www.britishjigsaw puzzlelibrary.co.uk.

British Model Flying Association (BMFA) is responsible nationally for all types of model flying, now the world's most popular aviation sport. It organises competitions and fun-fly meetings, provides advice and guidelines on model flying, offers third party insurance and can put you in touch with clubs in your area from its list of over 700 clubs. Many older members specialise in indoor free-flight or radio-controlled flying. Membership (2008) is £22 a year for senior citizens, which includes third-party liability insurance cover. Contact: Tel: 0116 244 0028; e-mail: admin@bmfa. org; website: www.bmfa.org.

Miniature Armoured Fighting Vehicle Association (MAFVA) is an international society that provides advice and informa-tion on tanks and other military vehicles and equipment, issues a bi-monthly magazine, *Tankette*, and can put you in touch with a local branch or overseas members with similar interests. There are meetings, displays and competitions. Membership in the United Kingdom (2008) is £9. Contact: Tel: 01477 535 373; e-mail: lloydstaples@btopenworld.com; website: www.mafva.net.

National Association of Flower Arrangement Societies. NAFAS can put you in touch with local clubs and classes but it is now also able to offer individual Affiliated Membership through a yearly subscription. The Association was formed 49 years ago and has a membership of over 70,000. The structure of the membership was formed through members belonging to one of the existing clubs within the 21 existing geographical areas of NAFAS. Lifestyles have changed and a number of people who would benefit from membership are unable to commit to club membership but are still interested in the work of NAFAS and floral art and design. The yearly subscription, which for 2008 is £35, includes four issues of *The Flower Arranger* magazine, 2 newsletters, details of NAFAS events, information on the National Show and details of NAFAS courses in Floral Art & Design including a home-study course. For further information contact: Tel: 020 7247 5567; e-mail: flowers@nafas.org.uk; website: www.nafas.org.uk.

National Philatelic Society. If you are interested in stamp collecting, you might like to join the National Philatelic Society. As a member, you can buy and sell stamps through their auctions or postal packet scheme. Members also receive invitations to monthly Saturday afternoon meetings, get a free bi-monthly magazine, *Stamp Lover*, and can borrow books from the Society's extensive library.

Membership costs from £23 a year. For further information, contact: Tel: 020 7239 2571; e-mail: nps@ukphilately.org. uk; website: www.ukphilately.org.uk.

Railway Correspondence & Travel Society. The Society is among the leading railway enthusiast groups, with nearly 4,000 members all over the country. Members receive the monthly magazine, *The Railway Observer*, which includes the Society's fixtures. There are regular meetings at about 30 centres and the Society has a library with postal loan facility. Membership (2008) costs £21 a year. Contact: Tel: 01242 523 917; e-mail: renewals@rcts.org; website: www.rcts.org. uk.

Railway Modeller is a magazine for railway enthusiasts. It lists railway preservation events and gives information about local railway societies – including how to contact them. £3 monthly.

Museums

Most museums organise free lectures, guided tours, and sometimes slide shows, on aspects of their collection or special exhibitions. As with art galleries and theatres, an increasing trend is to form a group of 'Friends' who pay a membership subscription to support the museum and in return enjoy certain advantages, such as access to private views, visits to places of interest, receptions and other social activities.

British Association of Friends of Museums (BAFM) is an umbrella organisation that acts as a national forum for Friends and volunteers who support museums around the United Kingdom. It shares news, provides advice on good practice, holds regional meetings and also produces a number of publications including a Handbook on setting up and running a Friends' organisation. Many museums offer the opportunity, through membership of a Friends' group, of rewarding voluntary activity. If you like the idea, enquire locally or contact the Association to discover what scope exists in your area. Individual membership (2008) is £15; group subscription rates vary depending on size of group. Contact: BAFM by e-mail: admin@bafm.org.uk; website: www.bafm.org.uk.

British Museum Friends. Members enjoy free entry to exhibitions and evening openings as well as information about lectures, study days and 'visits behind the scenes'. A mailing including the events programme and the *British Museum Magazine* is sent three times a year. Individual membership (2008) is £45. Contact: Tel: 020 7323 8195; e-mail: friends@britishmuseum.org. website: www.britishmuseum. org.

Friends of the Fitzwilliam Museum receive regular mailings with information about museum events including exhibitions, concerts, lectures and parties. There are visits to other museums and historic houses in the Cambridge area and throughout the United Kingdom, and trips to overseas cities are also arranged. Another attractive way of meeting other Friends is to become a voluntary helper at the museum. For membership details contact: Tel: 01223 332900; e-mail: fitzmuseum-friends@lists.cam.ac.uk; website: www. fitzmuseum.cam.ac.uk.

Friends of the National Maritime Museum. The museum complex, housed in Greenwich Park, comprises the largest maritime museum in the world, Wren's Royal Observatory and Inigo Jones's Queen's House. Friends enjoy free entry to the buildings and exhibitions as well as private views, lectures, astronomy and art clubs, sailing trips (for all abilities), visits to exhibitions and places of interest both in Britain and abroad, and a regular glossy magazine. There are reciprocal free entry arrangements with many other maritime organisations. Subscription rates (2008) are £40 individual membership; £55 for a family or joint membership; £28 concessions. Contact: Tel: 020 8312 6678; e-mail: membership@nmm.ac.uk; website: www.nmm.ac.uk.

Membership of the National Museums of Scotland. Members receive regular mailings and the *Explorer* magazine, invitations to lectures and other events plus free admission to exhibitions and some sites. There is also a United Kingdom and overseas travel programme. Annual membership (2008) is £23; £32 for couples. Contact: Tel: 0131 247 4191; e-mail: membership@nms.ac.uk; website: www.nms.ac.uk.

Friends of the V&A (Victoria and Albert Museum). Members enjoy free admission to V&A exhibitions, members' previews, a programme of events and a free subscription to *V&A Magazine*. Annual membership (2008) starts at £40 (£35 for over-60s). Contact: Tel: 020 7942 2271; e-mail: membership@vam.ac.uk; website: www.vam.ac.uk.

Nature and conservation

Many conservation organisations are very keen to recruit volunteers. By the same token, many of those concerned with field studies arrange courses and other special activity interests. The potential list is enormous. To give you a taste of what is on offer, this is a truncated list ranging from canals to ecology.

Amenity organisations. If you are interested in conservation and the environment, you may like to join your local amenity society. You should be able to contact it through your public library, or for a comprehensive list consult the website: www.handbooks.btcv.org.uk.

The Civic Trust is an environmental charity concerned with the quality of urban living, and acts as an umbrella organisation for a network of 850 local societies. The Trust coordinates Heritage Open Days and publishes a quarterly newsletter, with articles on planning, conservation and transport issues. Annual membership (2008) is £20, joint £25. Contact: Tel: 020 7539 7900; website: www.civictrust.org.uk.

Epping Forest Field Centre. This Field Studies Council Day Centre promotes 'bringing environmental understanding to all' through a wide-ranging programme of courses that take place both during the week and on many weekends of the year. Facilities include wheelchair access and a specially designed wheelchair path into the forest. Contact: Tel: 020 8502 8500; e-mail: enquiries.ef@field-studies-council.org; website: www.field-studies-council.org.

Forestry Commission. For details of walks and trails, forest drives, picnic places, wildlife watching and visitor centres, contact your local Forestry Commission office or the Public Enquiries service: Tel: 0845 367 3787; website: www. forestry.gov.uk.

Scottish Inland Waterways Association. The Association coordinates the activities of local canal preservation societies and will put you in touch with your nearest group. Individual membership is £5. Contact: Tel: 0131 229 8796; email: secretary@siwa.org.uk; website: www.siwa.org.uk.

The Wildlife Trusts. There are 47 local Wildlife Trusts caring for 2,500 nature reserves and campaigning for the future of our threatened wildlife. If you would be interested in visiting the reserves, participating in some of the activities, such as guided walks or joining a work party – which could mean taking part in anything from scrub bashing to otter surveys – contact your local Trust. Membership (2008), which is optional, costs about £24 for an individual and £30 joint. It includes receipt of a magazine and events programmes. For further information, contact: Tel: 01636 677711; e-mail: enquiry@wildlifetrusts.org; website: www. wildlifetrusts.org.

Sciences and other related subjects

If astronomy fascinates you or you would like to understand more about meteorology (who wouldn't, given our uncertain climate!), there are several societies and associations that would welcome you as a member.

British Astronomical Association. The Association is open to all people interested in astronomy. Members' work is coordinated in such sections as Sun, Moon, Terrestrial Planets, Meteors, Jupiter, Asteroids, Historical, Telescope Making and so on. The Association holds meetings both in London and elsewhere and loans instruments to members. Membership (2008) costs £42 a year for individuals; £29 for those over 65. Contact: T: 020 7734 4145; email: office@ britastro.org; website: www.britastro.org.

Geologists' Association. The Association organises lectures, field excursions and monthly meetings at Burlington House, and members also receive a quarterly magazine. Subscription rates vary; individual membership (2008) is £40. Contact: T: 020 7434 9298; email: geol.assoc@bt internet.com; website: www.geologists.org.uk.

Royal Meteorological Society. The Society, which includes among its membership both amateurs and professionals, exists to advance meteorological science. Members and others may attend scientific meetings and receive the monthly magazine *Weather*. Membership (2008) costs £60 a year. Contact: T: 0118 956 8500; email: info@rmets.org; website: www.rmets.org.

Women's organisations

Although today women can participate in almost any

activity on equal terms with men, women's clubs and organisations continue to enjoy enormous popularity. Among the best-known are Women's Institutes, the Mothers' Union and Townswomen's Guilds.

The Mothers' Union (MU) is a Christian organisation, with over 3.6 million members in 77 countries, which promotes the well-being of families through practical work, policy and prayer. Membership is open to all baptised Christians who support the charity's objectives. Members can be involved in a wide range of projects within their local community as well as with a worldwide fellowship network. Contact: Tel: 020 7222 5533; e-mail: mu@themothersunion.org; website: www.themothersunion.org.

National Association of Women's Clubs. There are 212 clubs with a membership of 7,250 throughout the country. They are open to women of all ages and interests. Each club is self-governing, choosing its own meeting times and programme. Typical activities include crafts, drama, keep fit and talks from guest speakers covering a wide variety of subjects. There are outings to theatres and exhibitions and visits to places of interest, and some clubs arrange holiday groups in Great Britain and abroad. Many do voluntary service in their communities for the sick and elderly. Membership is £8.50 a year to head office, plus a small membership fee to the local club. Contact: Tel: 020 7837 1434; website: www.nawc.org.uk.

National Federation of Women's Institutes (NFWI). The WI is the largest national organisation for women, with nearly 215,000 members and 7,100 local WIs in England and Wales. Through its community ties and wide-ranging activities, it offers women both friendship and the opportunity to develop their skills and talents. The WI has its own residential college, Denman College, and also publishes a monthly magazine, *WI Life*. Membership is £28 per annum. Contact: T: 020 7371 9300; email: hq@nfwi.org.uk; website: www.womens-institute.co.uk.

National Women's Register (NWR) is an organisation of 400 groups of 'lively minded women' who meet informally in members' homes to enjoy challenging discussions. The groups choose their own topics and many also arrange a varied programme of social activities. Annual membership is £15. Contact: T: 0845 450 0287; website: www.nwr.org.uk.

Scottish Women's Rural Institutes. This is the Scottish counterpart of the Women's Institute movement. It has about 25,000 members of all ages who enjoy social, recreational and educational activities. There are talks and demonstrations, classes in arts and crafts, and discussions on matters of public interest. You can be put in touch with your local institute via the headquarters office. Contact: Tel: 0131 225 1724; e-mail: swri@swri.demon.co.uk; website: www.swri.org.uk.

If you live in Northern Ireland, contact the **Federation of Women's Institutes of Northern Ireland**. Tel: 028 9030 1506 / 9060 1781; website: www.wini.org.uk.

Townswomen's Guilds is an organisation committed to advancing the social awareness of all women, irrespective of race, creed or political affiliation. It has around 43,000 members in 1,100 Guilds across the United Kingdom who meet to exchange ideas, learn new skills and take part in a wide range of activities. Annual subscription (2008) is £26; associate membership £13. Contact: Tel: 0121 326 0400; email: tghg@townswomen.org.uk; website: www. townswomen.org.uk.

2

Sport

Retirement is no reason for giving up sport. On the contrary, it is an ideal time to get fit. Facilities abound and, unlike people with a nine to five job, you enjoy the great advantage of being able to book out of peak hours. To find out about opportunities in your area, contact your local authority recreational department or your sports/leisure centre.

Angling

Angling Trades Association. The Association promotes the interests of anglers and angling, including educational and environmental concerns. It can advise on where to find qualified tuition, local tackle dealers and similar information, as well as supply a number of useful leaflets. Contact: Tel: 024 7641 4999; e-mail: ata@sportsandplay.com; website: www. anglingtradesassociation.com.

Archery

Grand National Archery Society (GNAS). The Society is the governing body for archery in the United Kingdom. It will put you in touch with your nearest club, of which there are over 1,000 around the country. Most clubs provide coaching at all levels, including beginners' courses (covered by public liability insurance) for which they supply all equipment. The GNAS organises a full calendar of events and says many archers are still actively competing in their 70s, as the handicap system covers all abilities and enables disabled people to compete on equal terms. Club membership is approximately £100 a year for an adult, including affiliation fees. Contact: Tel: 01952 677 888; website: www.gnas.org.

Badminton

Badminton England is the sport's governing body in England. Many categories of membership are available, from supporters, through club and county players to the World Class squad. Most sports and leisure centres have badminton courts and give instruction, as do many adult education institutes. If you need advice, call Badminton England for a local contact. Annual membership (2008) is £8.90 for club members plus a small county fee; £15 for non-club members. Contact: Tel: 01908 268 400; website: www.badmintonengland.co.uk.

Bowling

Over the past years, bowling has been growing in popularity. Your local authority may provide facilities. Alternatively contact:

English Bowling Association. There are 2,600 local clubs, many of which provide instruction for beginners by qualified coaches. Some clubs have reduced rates for senior citizens. A national competition for age 55-plus singles and pairs is organised through clubs each year. If you decide to take up bowls, you are advised not to buy your equipment without advice from the club coach. Contact: Tel: 01903 820222; website: www.bowlsengland.com.

English Indoor Bowling Association. The EIBA is the governing body of indoor bowls for men in England. There are currently 340 clubs, many of which are open throughout the year. Some offer reduced rates for retired people. Coaching is available at most clubs and there are a number of national competitions for the over 50s and 60s. Contact: Tel: 01664 481 900; e-mail: enquiries@eiba.co.uk; website: www.eiba.co.uk.

English Women's Bowling Association is the national governing body for outdoor level green bowls for ladies in England. The mission statement is to promote, foster and encourage the sport of level green bowls wherever it is

played. Contact: Tel: 01926 430 686; e-mail: office@
englishwomensbowling.net; website: www.englishwomens
bowling.net.

Clay pigeon shooting

Clay Pigeon Shooting Association (CPSA). The CPSA is an
association of individual shooters and a federation of clubs.
As a member you have public liability insurance of £5
million, your scores are recorded in the national averages
and you can compete in national events. The Association
produces its own magazine, *Pull!*, which is distributed free
of charge to all members. There are other specialist booklets
available on most aspects of clay shooting. Individual
membership (2008) is £55 per year; £44 for veterans (60
and over). Contact: Tel: 01483 485400; e-mail: info@
cpsa.co.uk; website: www.cpsa.co.uk.

Cricket

The Brit Oval is home to the Surrey County Cricket Club
and one of the main venues for international and county
cricket. Club membership entitles you to a number of benefits, including free or reduced price tickets for the Members'
Pavilion to watch international matches as well as county
events. Contact: Tel: 08712 461100; e-mail: enquiries@
surreycricket.com; website: www.surreycricket.com.

England and Wales Cricket Board. If you want to play, watch or help at cricket matches, contact your local club or contact the ECB. They can put you in touch with your county cricket board and they also organise an over-50 County Cricket Championship. Contact: Tel: 020 7432 1200; e-mail: feedback@ecb.co.uk; website: www.ecb.co.uk.

Lord's Cricket Ground. You can enjoy a conducted tour of Lord's that includes the Long Room, the futuristic Media Centre and the MCC Museum, where the Ashes urn is on display. Price is £10 (£7 for senior citizens). There are three tours per day during the summer at 10 am, 12 noon and 2 pm. From November to March there are two tours per day at noon and 2 pm. These times are subject to variation and you are advised to check before making a special visit. Senior citizens can attend County Championship matches and the National League matches for half price. There are no concessions, however, for major matches and early booking for these events is recommended. Contact: Tel: 020 7616 8500; e-mail: reception@mcc.org; website: www.lords. org.

Croquet

Croquet Association. A growing number of local authorities as well as clubs now offer facilities for croquet enthusiasts. The Croquet Association runs coaching courses and can advise you about clubs, events, purchase of equipment and other information. Contact: Tel: 01242 242318; e-mail: caoffice@croquet.org.uk; website: www.croquet.org.uk.

Cycling

CTC (**Cyclists' Touring Club**) is the largest national cycling organisation. It offers members free third party insurance, free legal aid, colour magazines, organised cycling holidays and introductions to 200 local cycling groups. There is also a veterans' section. Membership (2008) costs £35 a year; £22 for people over 65. Contact: Tel: 0844 736 8451; e-mail: membership@ctc.org.uk; website: www.ctc.org.uk.

Darts

British Darts Organisation. Opportunities for playing darts can be found almost anywhere in clubs, pubs and sports centres. Contact: Tel: 020 8883 5544; e-mail: britishdarts org@btconnect.com; website: www.bdodarts.com.

Golf

English Golf Union is one of the largest sport governing bodies in England, looking after the interests of over 1,900 golf clubs and 740,000 members. It is a not-for-profit organisation run for the benefit of the game and its players. Contact: Tel: 01526 354 500; e-mail: info@englishgolf union.org; website: www.englishgolfunion.org.

Golfing Union of Ireland. Contact: Tel: 00 353 1 505 4000; e-mail: information@gui.ie; website: www.gui.ie.

Scottish Golf Union. Contact: Tel: 01334 466477; e-mail: sgu@scottishgolfunion.org; website: www.scottishgolf.org.

Welsh Golfing Union. Contact: Tel: 01633 436040; e-mail: office@golfunionwales.org; website: www.golfunionwales. org.

The National Golf Unions can provide information about municipal courses and private clubs, of which there are some 1,700 in England alone. Additionally many adult education institutes and sports centres run classes for beginners.

Swimming

Amateur Swimming Association (ASA). Coaching and 'Learn to Swim' classes are arranged by many authorities, which also make the pool available at various times of the week for older people who prefer to swim quietly and unhindered. The Association offers an award scheme to encourage greater proficiency in swimming and as an incentive to swim regularly for fitness and health. If you are already a fitness swimmer, you might like to join Swimfit, which gives members access to training programmes and stroke technique tips. For further details contact: Tel: 0871 200 0928; e-mail: customerservices@swimming.org; website: www.sportcentric.com.

Table tennis

English Table Tennis Association. Table tennis can be enjoyed by people of all ages and all levels of competence. It is played in community halls, church halls, clubs and many sports centres. Contact: Tel: 01424 722525; website: www. englishtabletennis.org.uk.

The Veterans English Table Tennis Society (VETTS) holds regional and national championships including singles and doubles events for over 40s, 50s, 60s and 70s. These attract increasing numbers of men and women who enjoy playing socially and competitively well into their retirement. Annual membership (2008) is £10; £5 for those over 65. For further information on VETTS contact the Membership Secretary: Tel: 01462 671191; e-mail: valmurdoch@advance-internet. com; website: www.vetts.org.uk.

Tennis

Lawn Tennis Association (LTA) facilities have been greatly improving and your local authority recreation department should be able to inform you. The LTA can give you information about anything to do with tennis, from advice on choosing a racket to obtaining tickets for major tournaments. Best advice is to contact the LTA: Tel: 020 8487 7000; e-mail: membership@lta.org.uk; website: www.lta. org.uk.

Vets Tennis GB promotes competitions for older players in various age groups from 35 to 80 years. Its website lists affiliated clubs, gives the results of their national championships (indoor, clay and grass courts) and also provides details of club, county and international events. Contact: Tel: 07774 264 169; e-mail: vw@vetstennisgb.org; website: www.vetstennis.gb.org.

Veteran rowing

Amateur Rowing Association (ARA). Veteran rowing as a sport is fast growing in popularity. Enthusiasts range in age from 31 to well past 80. Senior ARA membership (2008) is £44. For those who enjoy a competitive edge, there are special races and regattas with types of boat including eights, fours and pairs as well as single, double and quadruple sculling. Touring rowing is also on the increase and additionally there is plenty of scope for those who simply want the exercise and a pleasant afternoon afloat. Nearly all clubs welcome novice veterans, both male and female, and usually the only qualification required is the ability to swim. Coaching is provided and membership is normally in the range of £80 to £400 a year for some of the London clubs. For information about clubs in your locality, contact the ARA: Tel: 020 8237 6700; e-mail: info@ara-rowing.org; website: www.ara-rowing.org.

Walking

Ramblers' Association. Rambling can be anything from a gentle stroll to an action-packed weekend trek with stout boots and a rucksack. The Ramblers' Association provides a comprehensive information service on all aspects of walking and can advise on where to walk, clothing and equipment and organised walking holidays. There are 450 local groups throughout the country that between them organise hundreds of walks a week. Membership (2008) is £27 a year; £36 joint; £15 for those of limited means. Contact: Tel: 020 7339 8500; e-mail: ramblers@ramblers.org.uk; website: www.ramblers.org.uk.

Windsurfing

Seavets, which is affiliated to the Royal Yachting Association, aims to encourage the not-so-young of all abilities to enjoy the challenge of windsurfing. Events are organised throughout the country from March to October, providing recreational windsurfing and racing for enthusiasts aged 35-plus. Average membership age is 63. Additionally, Seavets raises money every year for the charity Research Into Ageing, which funds research into the disabilities of old age. Annual membership (2008) is £15 per household. For more information please email the Membership Secretary: e-mail: paulfet@aol.com; website: www.seavets.co.uk.

Yachting

Royal Yachting Association (RYA). There are 2,200 clubs affiliated to the RYA and more than 1,500 recognised training centres. The Association also provides comprehensive information services for boat owners and can give advice on everything from moorings to foreign cruising procedure. Membership (2008) costs £39 a year (£36 by direct debit). Contact: Tel: 0845 345 0400; e-mail: member. services@rya.org.uk; website: www.rya.org.uk.

3

Holidays

Holidays are so much better when you've retired. No longer do you need to plan months ahead in order to fit in with colleagues. You can avoid peak periods, which are almost invariably more expensive and crowded. You can enjoy real flexibility, in a way that is usually not possible when you are working. Why not take several mini breaks when you feel like it, or perhaps go away for a month or two at a time? One of the greatest things about retirement is the availability of concessionary prices. You can research cheaper fares and reduced charges for hotel accommodation.

For ease of reference, entries are listed under such headings as 'art appreciation', 'sport', 'self-catering holidays', etc. Inevitably, some organisations criss-cross several sections, but, to avoid repetition, the majority are only featured once in what, hopefully, is the most logical place.

At the end of the chapter there are general information sections with brief details about insurance, concessionary fares and other travel tips. Prices and some of the other detailed information, if provided, are as accurate as possible.

One of the big gains of reaching retirement age is the availability of cheap travel. Local authorities are now required to offer men, as well as women, concessionary bus fares. Since April 2008, bus travel out of peak hours is free both for disabled people and those over 60 anywhere in the country. Coaches, too, very often have special rates for older people and, as everyone knows, Senior Railcards, available to men and women over 60, offer wonderful savings.

Art appreciation

Many tour operators, clubs and other organisations that arrange group holidays include visits to museums, churches and other venues of artistic interest along with their other activities such as walking, bridge and general sightseeing. There is one that specialises in cultural tours and has been operating for a long time: Specialtours. Alternatively, if you enjoy the performing arts, you could spend several glorious days attending some of the music and drama festivals held in many parts of the country, as well as some of the famous festivals overseas.

Specialtours arranges accompanied cultural tours in association with numerous organisations, including the Art Fund. The costs include flight, hotels, most meals, travel within the country, guides and entrance fees. For further information contact the Administrator: Tel: 020 7730 2297; e-mail: info@specialtours.co.uk; website: www.specialtours.co.uk.

Festivals

There is a feast of music, drama and the arts. The most famous festivals are those held at Edinburgh and Aldeburgh. Over the years the number of festivals has been growing and they are now a regular feature in many parts of the country. To find out what is going on where, contact the Arts Council or your regional Arts Council office. Look in the national press or search the internet for lists of major festivals at home and overseas.

Aldeburgh Music Festival in Suffolk is held annually during June. A varied programme of classical and contemporary music and opera at Snape Maltings Concert Hall, Jubilee Hall and other local venues is complemented by exhibitions, talks, walks and films. There are also three other festivals, variously at Easter, during August and in October. In addition there is a year-round programme of concerts and masterclasses that are open to the public. For further details contact: Tel: 01728 687100; e-mail: enquiries@aldeburgh. co.uk; website: www.aldeburgh.co.uk.

Edinburgh International Festival is held every August. Details of music, theatre, dance, opera and other events are available from early April. For further information, contact: Tel: 0131 473 2020; e-mail: info@festivalsedinburgh.com; website: www.edinburghfestivals.co.uk.

Three Choirs Festival, held every year since the early 18th century between the three great cathedral cities of

Gloucester, Worcester and Hereford, is one of the world's oldest classical choral festivals. There is something for everyone at Three Choirs. For more information contact: Tel: 01452 529819; e-mail: info@3choirs.org; website: www.3choirs.org.

Arts and crafts

The focus here is on taking courses or just participating for the pleasure, rather than viewing the works of others. The choice includes woodcarving and other crafts, painting and music.

Benslow Music Trust provides exciting opportunities for music-making and appreciation, with a year-round pro-gramme of weekend and midweek courses for adult amateur musicians of all standards. The programme includes chamber music, choral and solo singing, music appreciation, beginner courses, jazz, solo and ensemble wind, orchestras, big band and early music. For further details contact: Tel: 01462 459446; e-mail: info@benslow.org; website: www. benslow.org.

Crafts Council aims to position the United Kingdom as the global centre for the making, seeing and collecting of contemporary craft. This is a growing industry and contributes to the UK's reputation as a world leader in creativity. The Council works with a strategic choice of part-ners to make contemporary craft exciting and relevant to the widest possible audience and promotes the teaching and studying of contemporary craft. Contact: Tel: 020 7806 2500; email: education@craftscouncil.org.uk; website: www.craftscouncil.org.uk.

West Dean College, housed in a beautiful mansion surrounded by landscaped gardens and parkland, organises short residential courses in contemporary and traditional crafts, the visual arts, photography, music and gardening – variously lasting from one to seven days. A typical programme includes: calligraphy, textiles, woodcarving, picture framing, blacksmithing, sculpture, drawing and painting, stained glass, willow work and many more. There are also 10 full-time Diploma programmes, including the conservation and restoration of antique furniture, tapestry weaving and musical-instrument making, all of which are validated by the University of Sussex. Contact: Tel: 01243 818210; e-mail: enquiries@westdean.org.uk; website: www.westdean.org.uk.

Coach holidays

Some of the coach companies organise holidays, as distinct from simply offering a mode of transport. Advice note from other holidaymakers: before embarking on a lengthy coach tour, try a few shorter excursions to see how you cope with the journey. Some people swear by the comfort, others find coach travel very exhausting.

National Express provides a scheduled coach network to over 1,000 destinations throughout the United Kingdom and also a wide choice of short-break holidays to most European countries. An attractive example is a London short break from about £85, including return travel and one night's accommodation with breakfast. Passengers aged 60-plus travel for half price but this does not include the hotel costs. For further details contact: Tel: 08717 818181; website: www.nationalexpress.com.

Historical holidays

Holidays with a particular focus on history are becoming increasingly popular. The choice includes battlefield tours, exploring famous archaeological sites of Britain and the highly imaginative 'production' at Kentwell Hall.

Holts Tours – Battlefield & History offer a choice of over 40 battlefield, historical and archaeological tours throughout the world. All are accompanied by a specialist guide-lecturer and local experts are also used. The 2008 programme included: Cyprus – Aphrodite's Island; Anglo–Zulu War; Normandy 1944; 1918 Commemorative Tour; The Indian Mutiny. Most tours are half-board in good-standard hotels with private facilities. Every effort is made to cater for single travellers, many of whom are women. Special group tours can be arranged. Contact details: Tel: 0845 375 0430; e-mail: info@holts.co.uk; website: www.holts.co.uk.

Kentwell Hall. Every summer Kentwell Hall in Suffolk re-creates a living panorama of what life was like during the Tudor period. Participants are required to provide their own costumes and to enter into the role of a character living at the time: for example, this could be a 16th-century cook or haymaker. You are expected to prepare yourself by reading and there are open days at Kentwell with briefing sessions. The event lasts for three weeks and participants can stay for one, two or three complete weeks. The only cost involved is the provision of a suitable costume. All meals are free and there is camping space available. Those requiring more comfort can book into one of the many local bed-and-breakfast hotels. Applications should ideally be made by end of February, at the latest. Contact: Tel: 01787 310207; website: www.kentwell.co.uk.

Mike Hodgson Battlefield Tours. Military historian Mike Hodgson has over 25 years' experience in organising guided coach tours for small groups (about 25 people) to visit European battlefields. Recent tours (variously between three and five nights) included Agincourt, Waterloo, Ypres, Somme, Verdun and Normandy. The cost is from about £250 for all travel, hotel accommodation, meals and guiding services. Contact: Tel: 01526 342249; e-mail: info@mhbattlefieldtours.co.uk; website: www.mhbattlefieldtours.co.uk.

Should you wish to visit a particular grave, the **Commonwealth War Graves Commission** will help you identify the exact location. Contact: Tel: 01628 634 221; website: www. cwgc.org.

Poppy Travel is the specialist travel arm of The Royal British Legion. This organisation has been arranging visits to battlefields, war cemeteries and memorials since the 1920s. Their background in Remembrance gives them a unique insight into the historical significance of destinations, which is then blended with their proven travel and holiday expertise. They now offer trips to almost every location where our Armed Services have fought. Poppy Travel has established an unrivalled reputation for a sympathetic approach and professionalism. Contact: Tel: 01622 716729; e-mail: info@poppy travel.org.uk; website: www.poppytravel.org.uk.

Overseas travel

Many of the big tour operators make a feature of offering special holidays designed for the over-55s. For fun, we have also included companies that specialise in arranging cruises and packaged motoring holidays, and also information about time-sharing. For up-to-date details, you should check the websites.

Explore Worldwide arranges more than 400 tours to over 130 countries. Accommodation varies from camping to modest hotels and rustic lodges. To view the wide range of holidays on offer, contact: Tel: 0845 013 1537; e-mail: hello@explore.co.uk; website: www.explore.co.uk.

Relais du Silence is a French group of independently owned hotels with a network of about 230 hotels throughout Europe, including Britain. They offer tranquil, rural settings in two-, three- and four-star comfort at reasonable prices, with good food and a family-like atmosphere. For more information, contact: Tel: 00 33 1 44 49 90 00; e-mail: info@relaisdusilence.com; website: www.relaisdusilence.com.

Saga Holidays are exclusively for people aged 50 and over. There is a large range of options worldwide, including ocean and river cruising (including Saga's own cruise ships, *Saga Rose* and *Saga Ruby*), safaris, short- and long-stay resort holidays and multi-centre tours. There is also a selection of special interest holidays, including gardens, music, walking and art appreciation. Saga Holidays are sold direct and not through a travel agent. For further information contact: Tel: 01303 771 111; website: www.saga.co.uk/travel.

Cruises

Cruises are an exotic option and appeal to many people. There are a great variety of programmes, and the following are recommended.

Fred Olsen Cruise Lines operates four ships with departures mostly from Dover, Southampton, Leith, Greenock, Liverpool, Newcastle and Dublin. Choices include a winter season of Caribbean fly-cruises from London and Manchester, as well as from regional airports on selected dates. Itineraries range from a two-night mini-cruise to a world cruise. Prices range from the modest to the luxurious. For further information contact: Tel: 01473 742424; e-mail: internet@fredolsen.co.uk; website: www.fredolsencruises.com.

Norwegian Cruise Line offers fly-cruise and stay holidays in the Caribbean, Alaska, New England and Canada, Bermuda, South America, Panama Canal, Hawaii, Mexico and Europe. For further information contact: Tel: 0845 658 8010; website: www.ncl.co.uk.

Carnival Group cruise brands include P&O Cruises, Cunard Line, Princess Cruises, Ocean Village and The Yachts of Seabourn. For further information contact: Tel: 023 8065 5000; website: www.carnivalukgroup.com.

P&O Cruises offer a wide range of destinations including two round-the-world cruises, the Mediterranean, Atlantic Isles, the Baltic and the Caribbean. For further information contact: Tel: 0845 678 0014; e-mail: reservations@po cruises.com; website: www.pocruises.com.

Princess Cruises. Choose from 17 ships cruising to Alaska, the Far East and Australia, the Caribbean, Panama Canal, Mexico, South America, Hawaii and the South Pacific, New England, the Mediterranean and Scandinavia. For further information contact: Tel: 0845 3 555 800; e-mail: enquiry@ princesscruises.co.uk; website: www.princess.com.

Cargo Ship Cruises. If price is one of the main considerations and you don't mind sacrificing the dressing-up and organised activity, a happy solution could be to travel via cargo ship. Accommodation and facilities (there is often a swimming pool) vary according to the size and type of vessel, which could be a roll-on, roll-off container or a banana boat going to South America and back. A few of the best are:

Andrew Weir Cruises Tel: 020 7575 6480; website: www.aws.co.uk.

Cargo Ship Voyages Tel: 01473 736 265.

Strand Voyages Tel: 020 7766 8220; e-mail: voyages@ strandtravel.co.uk; website: www.strandtravel.co.uk.

Page & Moy Ltd. Choosing the cruise most likely to offer what you want no longer entails elaborate detective work if you consult tour operator Page & Moy. Discounts are offered on every booking and there are also many exclusive special offers. Cruise specialists are available seven days a week to give assistance. For further information contact: Tel: 08708 334012; website: www.pageandmoy.com.

Motoring holidays abroad

A number of organisations – including in particular some ferry operators – offer 'packages' for the motorist that include ferry crossings, accommodation and insurance. Although these often provide very good value, some people prefer to make all their own arrangements in order to get exactly what they want. Whatever your preference, if a main concern is carefree motoring, maybe one of the options suggested below could provide a happy solution.

Automobile Association. The AA offers several helpful products and services for motoring at home and abroad, including route planning, maps, AA Five Star Europe Breakdown Assistance and travel guides. For further details: Tel: 0870 600 0371; website: www.theaa.com.

Brittany Ferries offers short-break holidays in France and Spain including accommodation, breakfast and return car-ferry crossings. There is also a selection of gites holidays in France. For further details, contact: Tel: 0871 244 0744; website: www.brittany-ferries.co.uk.

RAC Motoring Services. As well as motoring breakdown cover for Europe, the RAC offers a range of overseas single trip or annual travel insurance, plus international driving permits, camping cards and other essential documents. For further details, contact: Tel: 08705 722 722; website: www.rac.co.uk.

Tips when motoring abroad. All basic common sense but, given the tales of woe one hears, many holidaymakers forget the obvious precautions:

▦ Have your car thoroughly serviced before you go.

▦ Take the following with you: a tool kit, manual for your car, a rented spares kit, a fuel can, a mechanic's light that plugs into the cigarette lighter socket and at least one extra set of keys.

▦ Always lock your car and park it in a secure place overnight (nearly 75 per cent of luggage thefts abroad are from cars).

Unless you are taking one of the packages that include insurance, you should contact your insurance company or broker well ahead of time to arrange special insurance cover. The ABI information sheet *Holiday Insurance and Motoring Abroad* summarises the essentials you need to know when taking your car overseas. Contact either the AA or RAC overseas-travel department. Both have facilities for helping you if you become stranded, and welcome non-members. See:

Association of British Insurers Tel: 020 7600 3333; e-mail: info@abi.org.uk; website: www.abi.org.uk.

Europ Assistance Tel: 0844 338 5533; e-mail: customer services@europ-assistance.co.uk; website: www.europ-assist ance.co.uk.

Green Flag Tel: 0845 246 1557; e-mail: member-queries@ greenflag.com; website: www.greenflag.com.

Advice from seasoned travellers is to have information

about garages, spare parts and the legal rules of the country, or countries, through which you are driving. The requirements – and documents you need to carry – are not the same for all European countries and failure to produce the right bond or special permit could mean a fine, or even imprisonment.

If your main purpose in taking your car is to enjoy the freedom it offers when you reach your destination, rather than the journey itself, it is worth looking at the Motorail facilities to Southern France and Italy and the long-range ferries to Spain and Portugal, which save on wear and tear and may be no more expensive than the extra cost of petrol plus overnight stays.

If instead of taking your own car, you plan to hire a car or motor scooter overseas, you will probably have to buy special insurance at the time of hiring the vehicle. Make sure that this is properly comprehensive (check for any excesses or exclusions) and that at very least it gives you adequate third-party cover. If in any doubt, seek advice from the local motoring organisation as to the essential requirements – including any foreign words or terms you particularly need to understand before signing.

Short breaks

A very large number of organisations offer short-break holidays all year round, with special bargain prices in spring and autumn. Many British hotels have winter breaks from

November to April, when full board can be considerably cheaper than the normal rates. Likewise, many overseas travel operators slash prices during the off-peak seasons. Although the websites contain plenty of suggestions, including some glorious city breaks, for very best value (and often all the more fun for being unplanned) look in the newspapers and on the internet for last-minute bargains.

Timesharing

Timesharing is an investment in long-term holidays and, as with other investments, should not be undertaken lightly. The idea is that you buy the use of a property for a specific number of days each year, either for an agreed term or in perpetuity. Your timeshare can be lent to other people, sub-let or left eventually in your will. Most timeshare schemes allow you to swap your annual holiday week(s) for one in other developments throughout the world, via one of the exchange companies.

A week's timeshare will cost from about £7,000 to over £40,000 depending on the location, the size of the property, the time of year and the facilities of the resort. The average is around £7,500 for one bedroom (peak season). Main-tenance charges could cost another £250-plus a week and you should always check that these are linked to some form of cost-of-living index, such as the RPI, and ascertain – item by item – precisely what the charges cover. Another useful point to check is that there is an owners' association linked to the property.

Although the great majority of people enjoy very happy experiences, stories about unscrupulous operators still occur. You should be on your guard against dubious selling practices that, despite efforts by industry watchdogs, have not been entirely stamped out. You might like to check whether the operator is a member of the OTE (Organisation for Timeshare in Europe), represented in the United Kingdom by the Timeshare Council. The OTE is the regulatory body dedicated to promoting the interests of all who have a legitimate involvement in the industry. It offers potential buyers free advice and information and also has an arbitration scheme, run in conjunction with the Chartered Institute of Arbitrators, to handle complaints that are not resolved through its standard complaints-handling procedure. Contact: **Organisation for Timeshare in Europe**: Tel: 00 32 2 533 3061; e-mail: info@ote-info.com; website: www.ote-info.com.

Most reputable companies also belong to one of two worldwide exchange organisations:

RCI Europe Tel: 0845 60 86 363; website: www.rci.com.

Interval International Ltd Tel: 0844 701 4444; website: www.intervalworld.com.

Existing owners wishing to sell their property should be on their guard against unknown resale agents contacting them 'on spec' and offering, in exchange for a registration fee, to act on their behalf. Although some may be legitimate, the OTE has received complaints about so-called 'agents' taking money and doing nothing further. A telephone call to OTE will establish whether the company is a member body. If not, leave well alone. If you are actually seeking an agent, OTE can provide you with a list of reputable resale companies (please enclose sae).

Self-catering and other low-budget holidays

If you cannot quite manage to survive on a tenner a day, some of the suggestions in this section need hardly cost you very much more. This applies especially if you are camping, caravanning or renting very simple accommodation with friends. The list includes: farm cottages, hostels, university accommodation and other rentals of varying degrees of sparseness or comfort.

Camping & Caravanning Club offers a national network of nearly 100 high-standard club sites, most of which are open to non-members. There are, however, many advantages in joining the Club. Members receive several free publications, including the monthly magazine *Camping and Caravanning* and the *Big Sites Book*, which lists details of over 4,000 places where you can camp in the United Kingdom. The Club also offers members a wide range of services including an exclusive RAC breakdown and recovery scheme, insurance and an overseas travel service providing competitive ferry bookings and overseas site reservations. Members aged over 55 pay reduced fees on Club sites. Contact: Tel: 0845 130 7632; website:www.campingandcaravanningclub.co.uk.

Venuemasters is a consortium of university and college venues that let residential accommodation during the vacation periods and some other times of the year. Charges start from £17.25 for en-suite bed and breakfast. For further information contact: Tel: 0114 249 3090; e-mail: info@ venuemasters.co.uk; website: www.venuemasters.co.uk.

English Country Cottages Tel: 0870 0781 100; website: www.english-country-cottages.co.uk.

Holiday Cottages in Scotland Tel: 01738 451610; website: www.scottish-holiday-cottages.co.uk.

Country Cottages in Ireland Tel: 0870 0781 600; website: www.chooseacottage.co.uk.

The 'cottages' differ enormously in size, style and location and are variously capable of sleeping between 2 and 22. Many are available for long or short breaks all year round, with low out-of-season prices from November to March. There are many more sites to choose from listed on the internet.

Farm Stay UK Ltd. Many farms take paying guests, let holiday cottages or run sites for tents or caravans. Farm Stay members offer a range of high-quality accommodation, all Tourist Board inspected, plus a glimpse of life on a farm. The Farm Stay guide contains information on over 1,100 good-value farm holidays all over Great Britain and Northern Ireland. Bed-and-breakfast facilities are normally from about £18 upwards. Many farms provide an evening meal, if required. Self-catering cottages start at around £150. Contact: Tel: 02476 69 69 09; e-mail: admin@farm-stayuk.co.uk; website: www.farmstayuk.co.uk.

Individual Travellers Company Ltd offers a large range of self-catering holidays in France, Italy, Sicily, Spain, Mallorca, Portugal and New England (USA). Properties vary widely in price, size and amenities, from chateaux complete with swimming pools to modest but comfortable apartments. Some in Spain and Southern France are suitable for short or long winter booking. Travel, car hire and insurance can be arranged. Contact: Tel: 0845 604 3829; website: www.individualtravellers.com.

Landmark Trust is a building preservation charity that restores historic buildings and lets them for holidays. Prices vary considerably over the 183 available buildings. These include castles, timber and thatched cottages, moated properties, towers and follies. For further details contact: Tel: 01628 825925; e-mail: bookings@landmarktrust.org.uk; website: www.landmarktrust.org.uk.

M P Associates in Northampton specialises in low-cost, long winter holidays (three or four months) in Spain, Portugal and Tenerife. Accommodation varies from one-bed apartments to four-bed villas. Rents are reasonably nominal, but in exchange, visitors are expected to maintain the properties as they would their own homes. For further details contact: Tel: 01604 230505.

National Trust Holiday Cottages has a wide variety of holiday cottages and flats in many areas of England, Wales and Northern Ireland with varying accommodation for 2 to 14 people. Although they are very popular in the high holiday seasons, there are usually plenty of vacancies at other times of year. For more information contact: Tel: 0844 800 2070; e-mail: cottages@nationaltrust.org.uk; website: www.nationaltrustcottages.co.uk.

The National Trust for Scotland has a large number of holiday cottages available in all areas, as well as cruises. For further information contact: Tel: 0844 493 2108; e-mail: holidays@nts.org.uk; website: www.ntsholidays.com.

Dot Destination Farmhouses has over 100 farms and crofts in all areas of Scotland, plus a few farmhouses in England, which take guests for two nights or longer. DDF can also offer help with car rental and ferry crossings. Contact: Tel: 01890 751 830; e-mail: enquiries@dotdestination.co.uk.

YHA (England and Wales) Ltd welcomes people of all ages. There are over 200 youth hostels in England and Wales and over 4,000 worldwide. Most hostels provide a meals service, cycle storage, lounge areas and self-catering facilities. The accommodation ranges from shared rooms to private rooms with en-suite bathroom. Overnight prices vary according to the location and facilities. For further information, contact: Tel: 01629 592700; e-mail: reservations@yha.org.uk; web site: www.yha.org.uk.

Special interest holidays

This includes weekend courses and more formal summer schools, between them offering a huge variety of subjects. It also includes holidays in the more conventional sense, both in Britain and abroad, but with the accent on a hobby.

Centre for Alternative Technology features interactive displays and working examples of sustainable living, renewable energy, environmentally responsible building and organic gardening. It is open daily to the public throughout the year, except Christmas and mid-January. Short residential courses are held frequently, ranging from two to five days, and subjects covered include renewable energy systems, organic gardening, environmental building and green sanitation. Accommodation is in simple two- to six-person bedrooms; there are also a few single rooms. Pensioners and those on low incomes are charged less. Opportunities also exist for voluntary work during the spring and summer. For a week or fortnight, volunteers live and work as members of staff, gardening and maintaining the site. Volunteers pay about £10 a day towards bed and board. For further details contact: Tel: 01654 705950; e-mail: courses@cat.org.uk; website: www.cat.org.uk.

City & Guilds offer special interest day, weekend and summer school courses at many colleges and universities throughout the country. Choice of subjects is enormous, ranging from yoga to astronomy, creative writing to digital photography. Prices vary widely. For further information contact: Tel: 020 7294 2800; e-mail: learnersupport@ cityandguilds.com; website: www.cityandguilds.com.

Denman College is the WI's residential adult education college. It runs over 500 short courses (two, three and four nights) each year. The courses are open to both WI and non-members, and include full board and tuition. Most of the accommodation is in single rooms, many with en-suite bathrooms. Courses cover such subjects as art, antiques, IT, dance, drama, literature, crafts, aromatherapy and many others. For further information contact: Tel: 01865 391991; e-mail: info@denman.org.uk; website: www.thewi.org.uk.

Earnley Concourse is a residential centre near Chichester that holds weekend and week-long courses throughout the year on such subjects as arts and crafts, music, wildlife, computer studies, keep fit, yoga and others. Charges are from £195 for a weekend. For more details contact: Tel: 01243 670392; e-mail: info@earnley.co.uk; website: www. earnley.co.uk.

Field Studies Council (FSC) offers over 600 leisure and special interest courses at its 14 centres throughout the United Kingdom. The courses cover a wide variety of subjects, including walking, outdoor pursuits, ecology and conservation, botany, birds and animals, history and archaeology, painting and drawing, photography, crafts and traditional skills, and many other general interest activities.

The centres are based in the Lake District, Yorkshire Dales, Snowdonia, Shropshire, Pembrokeshire, Exmoor, South Devon, Suffolk, the North Downs, Epping Forest, County Fermanagh and the Scottish Highlands. The courses vary in length from a weekend to a week. For more information contact: Tel: 0845 345 4071; e-mail: enquiries@field-studies-council.org; website: www.field-studies-council.org.

HF Holidays Ltd offers walking and special interest holidays in a wide range of locations throughout Britain and abroad. The choice of activities includes golf, bridge, bowls, ballroom dancing, yoga, painting, photography, music-making and birdwatching. There are also discovery coach tours and holidays, with gentle rambles and excursions, for those who want a more leisurely break. The walking holidays range from easy walking to rock scrambling. Overseas destinations include France, Majorca, Malta, Switzerland, Italy,

Canada, the USA, New Zealand and Peru. For more details contact: Tel: 0845 470 7558; e-mail: info@hfholidays.co.uk; website: www.hfholidays.co.uk.

Mercian Travel Centre Ltd specialises in arranging bridge and bowling holidays to over 15 countries throughout the world, variously lasting from four nights to a fortnight. Mercian also arranges a wide choice of cruises. For further information contact: Tel: 01562 883 795; e-mail: JDowning@merciantravel.co.uk; website: www.mercian travel.co.uk.

Peak District National Park Centre for Environmental Learning offers weekend and week-long special interest breaks including: painting and illustration, natural history, bird watching, navigation, photography and rambling. Losehill Hall is set in beautiful countryside with comfortable single- and twin-bedded en-suite accommodation. Prices fully inclusive of meals, accommodation, transport and tuition. For further information contact: Tel: 01629 816200; email: enquiries.losehill@peakdistrict.gov.uk; website: www. peakdistrict.org.

Vegi-Ventures is a holiday tour company that specialises in catering for vegetarians, offering an attractive range of destinations in Britain, Europe and farther afield. Accommodation is chosen very much with the food in mind and is variously in hotels, special guest houses and retreat centres with their own cook. Holidays include: house parties, a week's walking and sightseeing in the Lake District, and three weeks' 'journey of a lifetime' in Peru with tour guide and half-board. Flights are willingly arranged but are not part of the package. For further details contact: Tel: 01760

755888; e-mail: holidays@vegiventures.com; website:www.
vegiventures.com.

Sport

Holidays with on-site or nearby sporting facilities exist all
over the country. However, if sport is the main objective of
the holiday, it is often more difficult to know where to apply.
The list that follows is limited to organisations that can
advise you about organised residential courses or can offer
facilities, rather than simply put you in touch with, say, your
nearest tennis club.

Sportscotland runs three national sports centres that offer
courses for all levels in sports such as golf, hill-walking,
skiing and sailing. For more information contact: Tel: 0131
317 7200; e-mail: library@sportscotland.org.uk; website:
www.sportscotland.org.uk.

Boating

One or two ideas for holidays afloat are included, as well as
organisations that offer serious sailing instruction.

Blakes Holiday Boating offers holiday boating throughout
all the main waterways of Britain and also in France and
Ireland. Basic boating tuition is provided for novices. Costs
vary according to season, size and type of accommodation.
Pets are normally allowed on British holidays. For holidays
abroad, Blakes will quote an inclusive price with travel

arrangements. For further information contact: Tel: 0845 268 0768; e-mail: bbh.enquiry@holidaycottagesgroup.com; website: www.blakes.co.uk.

French Government Tourist Office can provide information about houseboats and other craft for hire in France. For further details contact: Tel: 09068 244 123; e-mail: info. uk@franceguide.com; website: www.uk.franceguide.com.

Hoseasons Boating Holidays – choose from the Norfolk Broads, the Cambridgeshire Waterways, the Thames, and the canals of England, Scotland and Wales, as well as boating holidays in France, Belgium, Holland, Italy and Ireland. Prices vary, travel and insurance can also be arranged. For further details contact: Tel: 0844 847 1356; website: www.hoseasons.co.uk.

Royal Yachting Association (RYA) can supply a list of recognised schools that offer approved courses in sailing, windsurfing, motor cruising and power boating. For further information contact: Tel: 0845 345 0400; website: www. rya.org.uk.

Cycling

CTC organises cycling tours in Britain and overseas and can also provide a great deal of extremely helpful information for cyclists wishing to arrange their own holiday, including advice on accommodation and scenic routes. Organised UK cycle tours include hostel accommodation or bed-and-breakfast accommodation with evening meal. Overseas tours vary from a fortnight's camping in Southern France to three weeks' holiday in South Africa. CTC also offers members: free third-party insurance, free legal aid and introductions to local cycling groups. For further information contact: Tel: 0845 045 1121; e-mail: info@cyclingholidays.org; website: www.cyclingholidays.org.

Cycling for Softies. Susi Madron's Cycling Holidays offer over 50 holiday options in 10 regions of France from 3 to 14 nights, cycling between a network of small country hotels, with terrain varying from very easy to quite a few hills. Travel, which is extra, can be arranged. For further information contact: Tel: 0161 248 8282; e-mail: info@cycling-for-softies.co.uk; website: www.cycling-for-softies.co.uk.

Railways. Cycles are allowed on some trains. However, it is normally necessary to make an advance reservation and there is usually a small charge to pay. Best advice if you are hoping to take your cycle by rail is to ring National Rail Enquiries on Tel: 08457 48 49 50; website: www.national-rail.co.uk.

Golf

Many clubs will allow non-members to play on weekdays when the course is less busy, on payment of a green fee. (A telephone call to the Secretary before arrival is normally advisable.) Better still, if you can spare the time, many hotels around the country offer special golfing weekends and short-break holidays.

Lotus Supertravel Golf offers a wide choice of golfing holidays overseas. Favourite destinations include Florida, Spain and the Algarve in Portugal. For further information contact: Tel: 020 7459 2984; website: www.golf.supertravel. co.uk.

Rambling

Rambling features on many special interest and other programmes as one of the options on offer. Three organisations that specialise in rambling holidays are described below.

ATG Oxford. Forget staying in cheap hostels and lugging around a rucksack with all your possessions for a week. Walking ATG Oxford-style means staying in the most comfortable hotels in the area, having your luggage transported and enjoying the option of a ride on days when you feel like taking it easy. The emphasis is on visiting places of historical, cultural or artistic interest, exploring the scenic highlights and dining out on the best local cuisine. Groups are limited to a maximum of 16 and most holidays last between five days and two weeks, with Italy a favourite destination. Other choices include France, Turkey, Spain, the Czech Republic, India, South Africa and many others. There are also walking and cycling holidays for those who prefer to travel more independently, yet who would welcome the services of a local representative and having their luggage transported. For further details contact: Tel: 01865 315 678; e-mail: trip-enquiry@atg-oxford.com; website: www.atg-oxford.co.uk.

Ramblers Holidays Ltd organise guided walking tours at home and abroad, ranging in choice from just four or five hours a day relatively gentle exercise to maybe nine hours a day hard mountain trekking. Some trips focus on a special interest such as birdwatching or flowers or make a particular feature of visiting places of cultural interest. There is also a huge choice of destinations including New Zealand, North America, China, South Africa, the Far East and most of Europe. For further details contact: Tel: 01707 331133; e-mail: info@ramblersholidays.co.uk; website: www.ramblers holidays.co.uk.

Exodus offers a wide choice of graded walking holidays in Europe (from about four hours a day) throughout the year. Accommodation is in hotels and guesthouses and includes half-board. Costs vary depending on the country and time of year. Cross-country skiing holidays are also offered during the winter. For more information contact: Tel: 0845 863 9600; e-mail: sales@exodus.co.uk; website: www.exodus.co.uk.

Skiing

Ski Club of Great Britain runs skiing holidays in Austria, France, Italy, Switzerland, Canada and the USA for over-50s who have some skiing experience. The cost is from about £750 a week for half-board, travel and qualified leaders who accompany each group and will ski with you and offer advice, if wanted. Two weeks are also available. For further information contact: Tel: 020 8410 2000; e-mail: skiers@ skiclub.co.uk; website: www.skiclub.co.uk.

A disability, including blindness or even an amputated leg, need no longer be a bar to skiing, thanks both to the availability of special equipment and to the efforts of Disability Snowsport. This provides opportunities for people with a disability to participate in skiing and snowboarding. It is their goal to help the individual improve their quality of life and transfer the benefits that they gain from taking part to their everyday life. For more information contact: **Disability Snowsport UK**: Tel: 01479 861272; e-mail: admin@disabilitysnowsport.org; website:www.disa bilitysnowsport.org.uk.

Tennis

The Lawn Tennis Association (LTA) can provide details of residential courses at home and abroad. For more information contact: Tel: 020 8487 7000; email: contactus.content@ lta.org.uk; website: www.lta.org.uk.

For **other sporting holidays** see 'Tourist boards' (page 92). Their websites give lots of information on golfing, sailing and fishing holidays, pony trekking in Wales, skiing in Scotland and many others.

Wine tasting

Wine-tasting holidays are becoming more popular every year. The best guided tours ensure plenty of variety with a mix of visits, talks, convivial meals, free time for exploring and memorable tastings.

Arblaster & Clarke Wine Tours operates tours to: France, Spain, Portugal, Italy, California, Australia, Hungary, Chile, South Africa and New Zealand. Most of the chosen regions are places of interest in their own right, famous for their historic buildings or picturesque scenery. Guides accompany every tour and, though groups can be as large as 36, every effort is made to give personal attention and to create a friendly, informal atmosphere. For more information contact: Tel: 01730 263111; e-mail: contact@winetours. co.uk; website: www.winetours.co.uk.

Winetrails offers wine-tasting holidays, combined with walking or cycling, in France, Italy, Spain, Portugal, Hungary and many other countries. Most last between 6 and 12 days and groups are limited to a maximum of 14 people. Trips for independent travellers and private groups can also be arranged. Contact: Tel: 01306 712111; e-mail: sales@winetrails.co.uk; website: www.winetrails.co.uk.

Holidays for singles

There are a number of people, who, if being completely honest, admit they would rather not go on holiday if it means travelling alone. It wasn't all that long ago that single people, especially women over 50, were virtually ignored by the holiday industry. Over the past few years many of the 'special interest holidays' are ideal for those without a partner. The companies listed below have been in existence for a number of years and do not operate for the under-35s.

Just You organises worldwide escorted holidays, including cruises, for single travellers. Groups usually include around 20 to 30 people, with ages ranging from approximately mid-30s to 70-plus. All room prices are based on sole occupancy without single room supplement. There are optional pre-tour get-togethers, the evening before, on holidays flying from Heathrow and Gatwick. For more information contact: Tel: 0870 252 8080; e-mail: telesales@justyou. co.uk; website: www.justyou.co.uk.

Solo's Holidays specialises in arranging group holidays for single people, including a good selection for those aged 45-plus. A vast choice of special interests is catered for, including opera, golf, cruises, walking holidays and many others. All tours are escorted 24 hours a day and most hotels are 3- or 4-star, without single room supplement. For further details contact: Tel: 0844 815 0005; e-mail: travel-solos@solosholidays.co.uk; website: www.solosholidays.co. uk.

Travel Companions is an organisation for individuals aged 20 to 80 seeking a congenial companion with whom to go on holiday. All applicants complete a form online listing their special interests, the type of destination they have in mind, as well as other requirements, and Travel Companions will then put them in contact with like-minded people. All personal information is handled in strict confidence. Travel Companions emphasises that it is not a dating service and makes the point that people often prefer to travel with someone of their own sex. For further information contact: Tel: 020 8762 9933; e-mail: email@single-living.com; website: www.singleagain.co.uk.

Holidays for those needing special care

Over the past few years, facilities for infirm and disabled people have been improving. More hotels are providing wheelchairs and other essential equipment. Transport has become easier. Specially designed self-catering units are more plentiful and of a higher standard. Also, an increasing number of trains and coaches are installing accessible toilets. As a result of these improvements, many people with disabilities can now travel perfectly normally, stay where they please and participate in the entertainment and sightseeing without disadvantage.

Travel and other information

If you need help getting on and off a train or plane, inform your travel agent in advance. Arrangements can be made to have staff and, if necessary, a wheelchair available to help you at both departure and arrival points. If you are travelling independently, you should ring the airline and/or local station: explain what assistance you require, together with details of your journey in order that facilities can be arranged at any interim points, for example if you need to change trains.

A useful free leaflet is *Rail Travel for Disabled Passengers*, available from mainline stations.

There are also a couple of useful publications, listing a wide choice of holiday venues, where disabled travellers can go in the normal way but with the advantage of having special facilities provided.

The Disabled Travellers' Guide, by the AA, gives information on holiday accommodation suitable for disabled individuals and their families, together with advice on travelling in Europe. Contact: AA Disability Helpline on Tel: 0800 262050; website: www.theaa.com.

Holidays in Britain and Ireland, £14.50, available from the Royal Association for Disability and Rehabilitation: Tel: 020 7250 3222; website: www.radar.org.uk.

A number of organisations provide rent-assisted (or sometimes free) holidays for the financially needy. Local Citizens Advice Bureaux, Age Concern groups and county branches of the British Red Cross will often know what, if anything, is available to residents in the area.

Tourism for All, formerly known as Holiday Care, can provide details about a wide range of accessible accommodation, facilities and services both in the United Kingdom and overseas. It also has information about hiring equipment for holiday use, accessible attractions and respite care centres, plus a list of hotels that offer substantial discounts. For further information contact: Tel: 0845 124 9971; e-mail: info@tourismforall.org.uk; website: www.tourismforall.org.uk.

ATS Travel. If, rather than simply wanting someone to point you in the right direction, you are looking for an agency that can make all the practical arrangements, get on to ATS Travel. This organisation specialises in planning tailor-made holidays for people with disabilities. Among other services, they will arrange the journey from door to door. This includes booking suitable accommodation according to your requirements. They will also organise the provision of special equipment and generally take care of any other details to make your holiday as enjoyable and trouble-free as possible. For further information, contact **ATS Travel**: Tel: 01708 863198; e-mail: aatstravel@aol.com; website: www.assistedholidays.com.

Another company that has been much recommended, especially for America, is **Virgin Holidays**. Winners two years running of the EASE awards, as the best tour operator for travellers with disabilities, they offer a wide range of hotels with wheelchair-accessible rooms, will arrange transport including adapted cars for hire and (subject to availability) will also book whatever medical equipment may be needed in-flight and during the holiday stay. For further information, contact: Tel: 0870 990 8350; e-mail: customer.care@virginholidays.co.uk; website: www.virginholidays.co.uk.

Many local Age Concern groups are a mine of information. They can often put individuals in touch with organisations that can assist with, say, transport or that organise special-care holidays, as do a number of Age Concern groups themselves. Age Concern England also publishes a free information sheet, *Planning a Holiday*, available from **Age Concern**: Tel: 0800 00 99 66; website: www.ageconcern.org.uk.

Another source to contact is your local social services department. Some local authorities arrange holidays or give financial help to those in real need.

Tourist boards

England's regional tourist boards and the Scottish and Wales tourist boards are the main sources of information for all aspects of holidays in their areas. They can advise about: accommodation, transport, highlights to see, special events and festivals, sporting facilities, special interest holidays – in short, almost everything you could possibly want to know. All produce excellent leaflets and guide books.

Visit Scotland. For further information, contact: Tel: 0845 22 55 121; website: www.visitscotland.com.

Wales Tourist Board. For further information, contact: Tel: 08708 300 306; website: www.visitwales.co.uk.

Regional tourist boards. Details of England's regional tourist boards are:

East of England Tourism. Covering Cambridgeshire, Essex, Hertfordshire, Bedfordshire, Norfolk and Suffolk. For further information, contact: Tel: 01284 727470; website: www.visiteastofengland.com.

Visit London. Covering the Greater London area. For further information, contact: Tel: 020 7234 5800; website: www.visitlondon.com.

North East Tourist Board. Covering the Tees Valley, Durham, Northumberland and Tyne & Wear. For further information, contact: Tel: 08701 601 781; website: www.visit northeastengland.com.

Tourism South East. Covering Berkshire, Buckinghamshire, East Sussex, Hampshire, Isle of Wight, Kent, Oxfordshire, Surrey and West Sussex. For further information, contact: Tel: 023 8062 5400; website: www.visitsoutheastengland. com.

South West Tourism. Covering Bath, Bristol, Cornwall, Devon, Dorset, Gloucestershire, Somerset, Wiltshire and the Isles of Scilly. For further information, contact: Tel: 01392 360 050; website: www.swtourism.co.uk.

Heart of England Tourism. Covering Birmingham, Herefordshire, Shropshire, Staffordshire, Warwickshire, West Midlands and Worcestershire. For further information, contact: Tel: 01905 761100; website: www.visitheartofengland.com.

Yorkshire Tourist Board. Covering Yorkshire and Northern Lincolnshire. For further information, contact Tel: 01904 707 961; website: www.yorkshire.com.

North West Development Agency. Covering Cheshire, Cumbria, Greater Manchester, Lancashire and Merseyside. For further information, contact: Tel: 01925 400100; website: www.nwda.co.uk.

East Midlands Tourism. Covering Derbyshire, Nottinghamshire, Lincolnshire, Leicestershire, Rutland and Northamptonshire. For further information, contact: Tel: 0115 988 8546; website: www.eastmidlandstourism.co.uk.

Long-haul travel

The two specialist organisations below can offer a great deal of practical information and help, as well as assist in obtaining low-cost fares, if you are planning to travel independently. Round-the-world air tickets are an excellent buy. Travel agents may also achieve savings by putting together routes using various carriers. Most airlines offer seasonal discounts that sometimes include a couple of nights' concessionary hotel stay, if you want to break your journey or visit another country at minimum extra travel cost.

Trailfinders Travel Centre will plan a tailor-made itinerary for you to any destination worldwide; book hotels, car hire and low-cost flights; and arrange comprehensive travel insurance. There is also a one-stop shop with information centre, visa and passport service, inoculation facilities plus guide books and handy travel accessories. For further information, contact Trailfinders travel: Tel: 020 7938 3939; first- and business-class travel: Tel: 020 7938 3444; European travel: Tel: 0845 050 5945; website: www.trailfinders.com.

WEXAS. As well as providing a comprehensive travel service for independent holidaymakers, WEXAS also offers a variety of trips to long-haul destinations, including such places as the Antarctic, China and the Nile Valley. Members enjoy flight, hotel and car-hire discounts and receive *Traveller* magazine. Those booking a long-haul flight economy class, plus at least two nights' accommodation through WEXAS, are entitled to VIP lounge access with their family at 23 UK airports. For further information, contact: Tel: 020 7589 3315; e-mail: mship@wexas.com; website: www.wexas.com.

Visa and passport requirements. All too many people get caught out at the airport by not keeping up-to-date with the visa and other requirements of the country to which they are travelling. These sometimes change without much warning and, at worst if you get it wrong, can result in your being turned away on arrival.

Health and safety advice sometimes also changes and travel agents are not always as good as they should be about keeping customers informed. Best advice, especially if you are travelling out of Europe, including to the United States, is to check the Foreign Office website – www.fco.gov.uk. – several weeks before departure, to allow time for inoculations, and again just before you leave.

Insurance

Even the best-laid holiday plans can go wrong. It is therefore only sensible to take out proper insurance cover before you depart. Regrettably, once you are over the age of 65, holiday insurance is not only more difficult to obtain but also tends to be considerably more expensive. However, were you unfortunate enough to fall ill or experience some other mishap, it would almost certainly cost you very much more than paying a bit extra for decent insurance. Eagle Star and Netcoverdirect are recommended as offering among the most competitive rates for older travellers.

Nevertheless, you are strongly recommended to shop around and get several quotes before paying for an unnecessarily expensive policy. For example, Help the Aged is enhancing its insurance policies for the over-60s and apparently will provide travel insurance up to any age. They currently have one customer aged 106 and will provide liability insurance for skiers in their 80s. Other firms who cater for people in their 60s and 70s are Halifax, American Express and Saga.

Many tour operators try to insist that, as a condition of booking, you either buy their inclusive insurance package or make private arrangements that are at least as good. Although this suggests that they are demanding very high standards, terms and conditions vary greatly. Before signing on the dotted line, you should read the small print carefully. Be careful to check that the package you are being offered meets all the eventualities and provides you with adequate cover should you make a claim. If, for any reason, you are unable to see an actual copy of the policy, ask any questions that you think might be relevant. This should include in particular any special conditions you would have to satisfy in making a claim (eg, are there medical conditions or possibly sporting/other activities that the policy would not cover).

If you are travelling independently, if anything it is even more important to be properly insured. Under these circumstances you will not be protected by the normal compensation that the reputable tour operators provide, for claims for which they could be held liable in the event of a mishap.

Holiday insurance should cover you for:

▨ medical expenses including: hospital treatment, cost of ambulance, air ambulance and emergency dental treatment, plus expenses for a companion, who may have to remain overseas with you should you become ill (see 'Medical insurance' page 102);

■ personal liability cover, should you cause injury to another person or property;

■ personal accident leading to injury or death (check the small print as some policies have reduced cover for older travellers);

■ additional hotel and repatriation costs resulting from injury or illness;

■ loss of deposit on cancellation (check what emergencies or contingencies this covers);

■ cost of having to curtail your holiday, including extra travel expenses, because of serious illness in the family;

■ compensation for inconvenience caused by flight cancellations or other travel delays;

■ cover for baggage and personal effects and for emergency purchases should your baggage be delayed;

■ cover for loss of personal money and documents.

If you are planning to take your car abroad (see 'Motoring holidays abroad', page 69), you will need to check your existing car insurance to ensure that you are properly covered. Alternatively, if you are planning to hire a car or motor scooter overseas, you will need to take out fully comprehensive insurance cover (which you may need to purchase while on holiday).

Before splashing out on new insurance, check whether any of the above items are already covered under an existing policy. This might well apply to your personal possessions and to medical insurance. Even if the policy is not sufficiently comprehensive for travel purposes, it will be better and cheaper in the long run to pay a small supplement to give you the extra cover you need than to buy a holiday insurance package from a tour operator. This could be especially true if you are over 65, as many travel agents load premiums against older holidaymakers on the basis of more costly medical insurance.

A cost-effective plan may be to extend any existing medical insurance to cover you while abroad. Then take out a separate policy (without medical insurance) to cover you for the rest of your travel needs.

Although many travel agents would like you to believe otherwise, **you are under no obligation to buy insurance from a travel company**. For a number of years, travel companies have not been able to oblige customers to buy their insurance as a condition of obtaining a special deal or discount. Also, whereas most companies selling insurance now need to be authorised by the FSA, this does not apply to travel insurance when bought as part of a holiday package from a tour operator or travel agent.

When assessing holiday insurance, and especially inclusive packages, it pays to do a bit of mental arithmetic. Although at first glance the sums look enormous, the likelihood is that should you have to claim you will end up being out of pocket. A sum of £750 or even £1,000 in respect of lost baggage might well be insufficient if, as well as your clothes, you had to replace your watch, camera and other valuables.

The Association of British Insurers suggests the following guidelines in respect of the amount of cover holidaymakers should be looking for in their policy.

Cancellation or curtailment of holiday: the full cost of your holiday, as well as the deposit and any other charges paid in advance; plus cover for any extra costs, should you be forced to return early. Depending on the policy, cover is normally limited to a maximum of £5,000 per person.

Money and travel documents: £500. Some companies offer additional cover for lost or stolen documents. Normally there is a limit of £200-£300 for cash.

Luggage/belongings: £1,500 (**NB**: check the limit on single articles).

Delayed baggage: £100 for emergency purchases in case luggage is lost en route and arrives late.

Delayed departure. Policies vary greatly. A number pay around £20 to £30 if departure is delayed by more than a certain number of hours. Some will allow you to cancel your holiday once departure has been delayed by over 12 hours, with cover normally limited to the same as for cancellation. If risk of delay is a serious concern, you should check the detail of your policy carefully.

Personal liability: up to £2 million.

It is essential that you take copies of the insurance documents with you, as losses or other claims must normally be reported immediately. You will also be required to quote the reference number and/or other details, given on the docket. Additionally, there may be particular guidelines laid down by the policy; for instance, you may have to ring a helpline before incurring medical expenses. Failure to report a claim within the specified time limit could nullify your right to compensation. Best advice is to check that you have the 24-hour helpline number and to keep it with you at all times.

Be sure to get a receipt for any special expenses you incur – extra hotel bills, medical treatment, long-distance phone calls and so on. You may not get all the costs reimbursed but if your insurance covers some or all of these contingencies, you will need to produce evidence of your expenditure.

The Association of British Insurers publishes a free information sheet on holiday insurance and motoring abroad, explaining the key points you should know in simple language. For further information, contact: Tel: 020 7600 3333; website: www.abi.org.uk.

The Association of British Travel Agents operates a code of conduct for all travel agents and tour operators who are members of ABTA, and also runs a consumer advisory service for holidaymakers on how to seek redress if they are dissatisfied with their travel company. For further information contact: Tel: 020 7637 2444; website: www.abta.com.

Compensation for lost baggage. If the airline on which you are travelling loses or damages your baggage, you should be able to claim compensation up to a maximum value of about £850. (The figure may vary slightly up or down, depending on currency fluctuations.)

Also useful to know about is the **Denied Boarding Regulation**, which entitles passengers who cannot travel because their flight is overbooked to some immediate cash payment. This applies even if the airline puts them up in a hotel or books them on to an alternative flight a few hours later. To qualify, passengers must have a confirmed reservation and have checked in on time. Also, the airport where they were 'bumped off' must be in an EU country. (It may sometimes also be possible to get compensation in the United States.)

If as opposed to being overbooked, your flight is cancelled, you are entitled to get a refund if you decide not to travel. Alternatively, you can request to be re-routed. You may, additionally, get compensation of between £125 and £600, depending on the length of your journey and how long you are delayed. If the delay is more than two hours, you will also be entitled to meals/refreshments plus two free telephone calls, emails or faxes. If it is overnight and you have more than five hours' wait, you will be put up in a hotel and given free transfers. Compensation is not, however, obligatory if the cancellation is due to 'extraordinary circumstances which could not have been avoided'.

For further information, or if you have trouble in obtaining your compensation, contact the **Air Transport Users' Council** on Tel: 020 7240 6061; website: www.caa.co.uk.

If you **miss your flight or have to cancel your trip**, you may be able to get a refund on at least a small part of the ticket cost. Most airlines will reimburse non-fliers for the air passenger duty and overseas government taxes, This applies even to normal non-refundable tickets. However, you have to make a claim and in most cases there is an administration charge. This may vary somewhere between £15 and £20. If you booked through a travel agent, there could be a second administration charge. Even so, especially for long-haul travel and family holidays, the savings could be quite considerable.

Medical insurance

This is one area where you should never skimp on insurance. Although many countries now have reciprocal arrangements with the United Kingdom for emergency medical treatment, these vary greatly both in quality and generosity. Some treatments are free, as they are on the National Health Service; others, even in some EU countries, may be charged for as if you were a private patient.

The Department of Health leaflet *Health Advice for Travellers* (T7) explains what is entailed and what forms you should obtain. In particular you should get a European Health Insurance Card (EHIC), which has recently replaced the old E111 forms. In practice, you are unlikely to notice very much difference. Similar to the E111, the card entitles you to free or reduced-cost emergency medical treatment throughout EU countries, as well as in Switzerland, Norway, Iceland and Liechtenstein.

If you had a 2005 E111 form and ticked the relevant box, you should automatically have been issued with the new European card. If you have not received one, call: T: 0845 605 0707. If you are applying for a form for the first time, you should be able to obtain one from any main Post Office or download a copy from the Department of Health website: www.dh.gov.uk. Alternatively, contact: Tel: 0845 606 2030. Each member of the family requires their own individual card.

However, even the very best reciprocal arrangements may not be adequate in the event of a real emergency. Moreover, they certainly will not cover you for any additional expenses you may incur. These could include the cost of having to prolong your stay, extra hotel bills if a companion has to remain with you, special transport home should you require it and so on. Additionally, since in an emergency you may need or want private treatment, you would be advised to insure for this – even if you are going to a country where good reciprocal arrangements exist.

In the United States the cost of medical treatment is astronomical. For peace of mind, most experts recommend cover of £1 million for most of the world and up to £2 million for the United States. Some policies offer higher, or even unlimited, cover.

Most insurance companies impose various terms and let-out clauses as a condition of payment. You should read these very carefully because, whereas some are obviously sensible, others may be very restrictive or, for whatever reason, you may not be able to satisfy the requirements: for example, if you have a chronic heart condition. Even though this may result in your having to pay a higher premium, you should declare any pre-existing illnesses or conditions. Failure to do so could nullify your claim if you had to make one.

Although theoretically there is no upper age limit if you want to take out medical insurance, some insurance companies are very difficult about insuring older travellers. Many request a note from a qualified medical practitioner stating that you are fit to travel if you are over 75, or require you to confirm that you are not travelling against medical advice.

Another common requirement is that the insured person should undertake not to indulge in any dangerous pursuits, which is fine in theory but in practice (depending on the company's interpretation of 'dangerous') could debar you from any activity that qualifies as 'strenuous'.

Book through a reputable operator. Many of the sad tales of woe one hears could have been avoided, or at least softened by compensation. It is essential that holidaymakers check to ensure that their travel agent or tour operator is affiliated to either ABTA or to the Association of Tour Operators (ATO). Both organisations have strict regulations that all member companies must follow and both run an arbitration scheme in the event of complaints. No one can guarantee you against every mishap, but a recognised travel company plus adequate insurance should go a long way towards giving you at least some measure of protection.

Travel and other concessions

Buses, coaches, some airline companies and especially the railways offer valuable concessions to people of retirement age. Some of the best-value savings that are available to anyone aged 60 and over are provided by train companies. These include:

Senior Railcard. This costs £20 and entitles you to one-third off most fares including: Cheap Day singles and returns; Savers and SuperSavers returns and most Rail Rover tickets; first-class single and return tickets; and all-zone off-peak Travelcards, subject to a minimum fare. Discounts are also available on some ferry services for through rail/sea journeys. Tel: 08457 48 49 50; website: www.railcard.co.uk.

Family Railcard. This costs £20 and entitles up to four adults to one-third off most fares (including Cheap Day singles and returns, Savers and SuperSavers), when travelling with between one and four children aged 5 to 15. The children get 60 per cent off the normal child fare (subject to a minimum fare of £1). Under-5s go free. Tel: 08457 48 49 50; website: www.railcard.co.uk.

Disabled Person's Railcard. This costs £18 and entitles the holder and one accompanying adult to reduced train fares. Details and eligibility criteria are shown in the *Rail Travel for Disabled Passengers* booklet available from your local staffed station. Tel: 08457 48 49 50; website: www.railcard. co.uk.

Network Railcard. This costs £20 and is only available in South-East England. It gives a one-third reduction on most

Standard Class fares after 10 am, Monday to Friday, subject to a £10 minimum fare. The same reduction applies at weekends and bank holidays, when happily there is no minimum fare; also, passengers can travel at any time, as opposed to only after 10 am. Up to four adults (including the cardholder) can travel at a discount and up to four children aged 5 to 15 will get 60 per cent off the normal child fare (subject to a minimum fare of £1). Under-5s travel free. Tel: 08457 48 49 50; website: www.railcard.co.uk.

Railplus Cards. Available to persons from age 60 who are also British Senior Railcard holders. They cost £12 and entitle you to savings of up to 25 per cent on first- and standard/second-class full fares on cross-border journeys within Europe. Reductions on Cross Channel Seacats and ships are only allowed if these services are part of rail/sea combined tickets to or from the Continent. The cards also allow you to purchase discounted international tickets for cross-border travel on the Continent. Railplus Cards can be obtained via Rail Europe-appointed travel agencies, and International Rail, contact: Tel: 08700 84 14 10; e-mail: sales@international rail.com; website: www.internationalrail.com.

Buses and coaches

There are often reduced rates for senior citizens on long-distance buses and coaches. For example, discounts of 33 per cent apply on National Coaches on both ordinary and Rapide services. If you are planning to travel by coach, it is worth shopping around to find out what bargains are available.

Airlines

Several of the airlines offer attractive discounts to older travellers. The terms and conditions vary, with some carriers offering across-the-board savings and others limiting them to selected destinations. Likewise, in some cases the qualifying age is 60; in others, it is a couple of years older. A particular bonus is that concessions are often extended to include a companion travelling at the same time.

These discounts are not particularly widely advertised and may well not be suggested by airline staff, often because they do not know a passenger's age. Best advice is to ask your travel agent or the airline at time of booking what special discounts, if any, are offered.

Overseas

Many countries offer travel and other reductions to retired holidaymakers, including, for example, discounts for entry to museums and galleries, and for day excursions, sporting events and other entertainment. As in Britain, provisions are liable to change and for up-to-date information probably the best source to contact is the national tourist office of the country to which you are travelling. All EU countries – as well as most lines in Switzerland – give 25 per cent reductions on international rail fares. These are available to holders of a Railplus Card purchasing international rail travel tickets and are applicable to both first- and second-class travel.

Air Travel Advisory Bureau advises on travel insurance and low-cost fares to all parts of the world. If you are looking for good-value fares, it is well worth contacting them. For further information: Tel: 01892 55 34 35.

Airport meet-and-greet services. An extravagance, admittedly. But if you hate the hassle of parking your car in the long-term car park and collecting it again on your return after a long journey, then a firm that will do the job for you could be worth paying for. BCP, which operates a meet-and-greet service at six airports (Heathrow, Gatwick, Stansted, Birmingham, Manchester and Edinburgh), will arrange for a rep to meet you at the terminal at both ends of your journey, park the car, deliver it back and, if you would like them to do so, give it a car-wash while you are on holiday. Price varies according to how long you will be away and the particular airport charges. For further details: Tel: 0871 360 1013; e-mail: communications@parking-bcp.co.uk; website: www.parkbcp.co.uk.

A number of other firms offer a similar service, but whereas some are reputable, others are cowboy operators who park owners' vehicles on unauthorised sites, risking damage to the car or even its theft. As a basic precaution at time of booking, enquire where your car will be parked, and when dropping it off, it would be sensible to ask for a 'conditions form' to complete, to avoid disputes if you find any damage on your return.

Health tips for travellers

Most are plain common sense – but worth repeating for all that:

■ Remember to pack any regular medicines you require: even familiar branded products can be difficult to obtain in some countries.

■ Take a mini first-aid kit, including plaster, disinfectant, tummy pills and so on.

■ If you are going to any developing country, consult your doctor as to what pills (and any special precautions) you should take.

■ One of the most common ailments among British travellers abroad is an overdose of sun. In some countries, it really burns, so take it easy, wear a hat and apply plenty of protective lotion.

■ The other big travellers' woe is 'Delhi belly', which unhappily can occur in most hot countries, including Italy and Spain. Beware the water, ice, salads, seafood, ice cream and any fruit that you do not peel yourself. Department of Health advice is only to eat freshly cooked food that is thoroughly cooked and still piping hot.

■ Always wash your hands before eating or handling food, particularly if you are camping or caravanning.

■ Travelling is tiring and a sudden change of climate more debilitating than most of us admit. Allow plenty of time during the first couple of days to acclimatise before embarking on an activity programme that would exhaust a 17-year-old.

▓ Have any inoculations or vaccinations well in advance of your departure date.

▓ When flying, wear loose clothes and, above all, comfortable shoes as feet and ankles tend to swell in the air.

▓ To avoid risk of deep-vein thrombosis, which can be fatal, medical advice is to do foot exercises and walk around the plane from time to time. For long-haul travel especially, wear compression stockings, which can be bought at most chemists. Unless advised otherwise by your doctor, taking an aspirin before flying is also recommended.

▓ On long journeys, it helps to drink plenty of water and remember the warning that 'an alcoholic drink in the air is worth two on the ground'. If you have a special diet, inform whoever makes your booking. Most airlines, especially on long-distance journeys, serve vegetarian food.

▓ Department of Health leaflet T7, *Health Advice for Travellers* contains essential information and advice on what precautions to take when you travel abroad and how to cope in an emergency. Contact: Tel: 020 7210 4850; website: www.dh.gov.uk.

▓ Finally, the old favourite, don't drink and drive.

Summary

The preceding pages are packed full of information on activities of all kinds. There should be something here of interest to everyone, whether you wish to take up a hobby locally, do volunteer work, learn a new skill or travel to places that you've longed to visit. With some good advice on insurance and a checklist for those wishing to travel and remain healthy, you should be able to fill every available moment of your leisure time with an activity that is both absorbing and interesting. You will probably find life busier now than ever before.

Notes

ALSO AVAILABLE FROM KOGAN PAGE

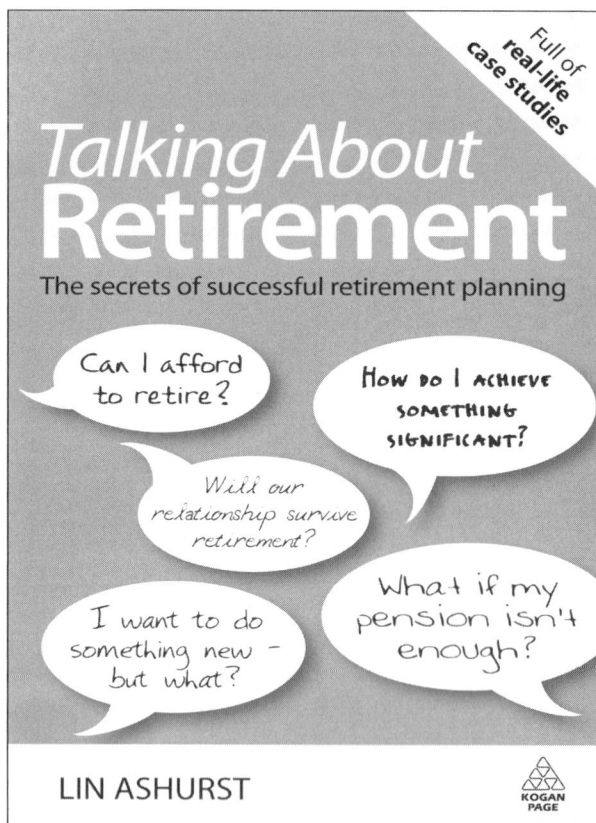

Order online now at www.koganpage.com

Sign up for regular e-mail updates on new
Kogan Page books in your interest area

ALSO AVAILABLE FROM KOGAN PAGE

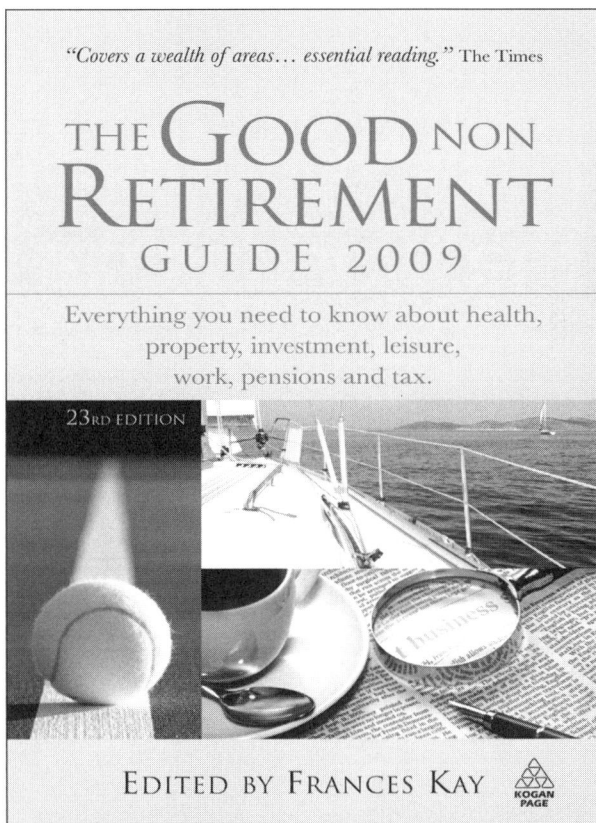

Order online now at www.koganpage.com

Sign up for regular e-mail updates on new
Kogan Page books in your interest area